solving conflict nonviolently

Atrium Society Publications
P.O. Box 816
Middlebury, VT 05753

Copyright © 1991 by Terrence Webster-Doyle
First printing 1991, Second printing 1992, Third printing 1992
Fourth printing 1993, Fifth printing 1994, Sixth printing 1995
Seventh printing 1996, Eighth printing 1997

Illustrations:	Rod Cameron
Cover Design:	Robert Howard
Design & Production:	Charlene Koonce
Typesetting:	I'm Your Type
Advisor:	John Shoolery
Creative Consultant:	Jean Webster-Doyle

Publisher's Cataloging in Publication Data
(Prepared by Quality Books, Inc.)

Webster-Doyle, Terrence, 1940–
       Why is everybody always picking on me?: a guide to handling bullies for young people / by Terrence Webster-Doyle; [illustrations, Rod Cameron].—p. cm.—(Education for Peace Series)
       SUMMARY: Stories and activities show how to resolve conflicts nonviolently. Constructive ways for young people to peacefully confront hostile aggression.
       ISBN 0-942941-22-5 (paperback)
       ISBN 0-942941-23-3 (hardcover)
       1. Bullying—Juvenile literature.   2. Conflict management—Juvenile literature.
       3. Nonviolence—Juvenile literature.   4. [Bullying] I. Cameron, Rod. II. Title.
       III. Series
BF637.B85   302.54
Library of Congress Catalog Number: 90-85197

Atrium publications are available at special discounts for bulk purchases, premiums, fundraising, or educational use. For details, contact:

Special Sales Director
Atrium Publications
P.O. Box 816
Middlebury, VT 05753
(800) 848-6021

Printed in Hong Kong

Special Thanks to Jean Webster-Doyle,
for her patient, loving support and understanding,
and for making this work possible.

WHY IS EVERYBODY ALWAYS PICKING ON ME?

A GUIDE TO UNDERSTANDING BULLIES
For Young People

by Terrence Webster-Doyle

An Education for Peace Book
published by Atrium Society
Middlebury, Vermont

This book is dedicated to you young people who have been bullied and who want to understand this problem and deal with it creatively. This book is also dedicated to you young people who bully others. I know you can benefit from healthy, peaceful ways to get what you need.

Table of Contents

Have you ever felt:

Anxious?	Helpless?
Worthless?	Powerless?
Out of control?	Unfairly punished?
Ridiculed?	Harassed?
Hurt?	Vengeful?
Ashamed?	Angry?
Humiliated?	Frustrated?
Insecure?	Lonely?
Enraged?	Unloved?
Rejected?	Violent?
Ambitious?	Greedy?
Pressured to conform?	Pressured to compete?
Scared?	Afraid of not "making it"?

Afraid of not living up to the expectations of others?

**In other words, have you ever felt
that everybody is picking on you?**

Boys Will Be Boys
A Story

Whack! You feel a sharp pain in your back. You spin around in anger to see the boy who threw the ball and hit you.

"Hey, you, Jack! I'll get you for that!" you yell at him, clenching your fists as you walk in his direction. Your palms sweat and your eyes harden as you approach this smaller and younger boy. "I could put your lights out for hitting me!" you say to him as you grab his shirt.

"I'm sorry! I didn't mean to hit you. It was an accident," the smaller boy says fearfully. He is so afraid of you, his body is shaking. You feel a surge of power from his fear. You know you are in control.

Other kids on the playground gather about you as you continue to harass this younger boy.

"Oh, sure. It was no mistake, punk. You're asking for a bruising!"

You feel the eyes of your classmates on you. You feel that they admire your strength, and fear it at the same time. Most of the kids keep away from you. The few buddies you have hang out with you because they also think bullying other kids is having a good time.

"Stop that, this minute!" you hear Mrs. Potter, the playground supervisor, command from across the yard. She is coming toward you at full steam, her finger wagging "Bad boy!" and her tone threatening the vice principal's office again.

"What a dope she is," you think to yourself. "She can't scare me. All the vice principal can do is send me home. Then what? No one's there and they don't care anyhow."

"Let go of Mark right now, or I'll send you to Mr. Nathan. You are a bully. Don't you think that you can get away with this behavior. I won't tolerate it. Why can't you be good, like Mark? He wouldn't start a fight; he has fine manners. You're a troublemaker, and you always will be as far as I'm concerned," she lectures.

Mrs. Potter puts her hand on your arm and you push it off. You let go of Mark to face Mrs. Potter. "You're not one of my parents. You can't tell me what to do," you yell back at her defiantly, your hands on your hips, your feet apart.

"Come with me. We are going to the vice principal's office right now," she insists.

"No way. I'm out of here!" You run across the yard and to the field beyond the school, yelling names back at the playground supervisor and the group of kids that are standing around. "Jerks, punks! I'll get you yet! All of you! You wait and see!"

After school you meet your two buddies, Mac and Tom. You hang out behind the stores downtown in the empty lot where you throw rocks at bottles and smoke cigarettes that you stole from your parents.

It's getting dark and your buddies and you start to go home. As you arrive at your house, your mother pulls up in her new, expensive foreign car. Your dad is still at work, as usual. Both of them work six days a week, usually into the late evening hours. Walking into the house, you see your big sister crashed out on the sofa, eating pizza and watching TV.

"Hey, weirdo. How goes it?" she sneers. "Failing all your subjects as usual?" You don't respond. "Got into a fight today, I heard."

"Aw shut up," you snap back at her, heading into the kitchen to see what you can find to eat.

"You're going to end up a bum or a convict, if you don't watch out, you know," your sister yells with a mouth full of doughy pizza. "You're just too dumb to learn. You're going to flunk everything if you don't straighten out, ya' hear me?"

You get some leftover pizza, a coke and some chocolate doughnuts and go into the living room to watch TV. Your mother has gone into her office upstairs to make some phone calls.

"Change the channel," you command your bigger sister with a look of anger. "I want to watch 'Rambo IV' and it's on now."

"You always watch that macho junk," your sister says, not looking at you, and not changing the channel. "You should watch something more intelligent instead of all that war stuff. It'll pollute your brain." She looks at you. "Maybe it's too late. Your brain has turned to mush already. Why can't you be more like Jason? He gets good grades and everyone likes him. He's a better brother than you," she says, smugly. "Did you hear he's getting a football scholarship to State?"

"Jason's a fake. He wants to be just like Dad, a big success. But he's just a phony. You think I'm a bully? So is he. But he's sly like a fox. He sweet-talks all his teachers. They'd do anything for him. He's just like the rest of those phony jocks he hangs out with. They're all alike. They play the same game, and I'm not talking about football. They get into college and get all the big-time lawyer, banker, stock market jobs. They're all phonies. But try to get in their way and they'll knock you over. Rambo's nothing but mush compared to those guys. Talk about aggressive! But everyone loves them for it, because they're playing the success game."

(Secretly, you are jealous of your brother, because your Mom and Dad always seem to favor him. When you and Jason were younger, he used to beat you up a lot. He *really* hurt you. When you told Mom and Dad, Jason would lie and say that you started it. You always got the blame and Jason usually got off with a slight reprimand. "Boys will be boys," your father used to say, patting Jason on the back while giving you a disapproving look. The memory fuels your anger and you're boiling inside.)

"Change the channel before I give you one," you threaten your sister. She knows you mean business.

"I might as well. You probably can't understand this program anyhow. Your level of mentality is just above a cave man's. You can't even talk intelligently. No wonder you don't have any friends — only those jerks, Mac and Tom. You'll all land up in jail together someday."

Your sister gets up to leave. You notice how overweight she is. She never gets any exercise. She eats way too much junk food and reads trashy movie magazines. She looks at you with contempt. "All that those G.I. Joe characters do is grunt. No wonder you understand them," she says coldly as she turns her back on you to leave the room.

You make a rude face and turn your attention to the movie. Rambo has just been trapped in the jungle and is fighting his way past the enemy patrol. He is big and harsh looking, with his M-16 gun spraying bullets everywhere. With a defiant scream, he throws a grenade at the oncoming "gooks," blowing them up.

Suddenly he is jumped from behind by one of the patrol. You watch Rambo fight in hand-to-hand combat with this violent looking creature.

They roll down into the river, where they continue to punch, kick, and strike at each other. Rambo grabs the enemy by the throat and holds him underwater with a look of crazed intensity on his face. Finally Rambo pulls out his commando knife and plunges it beneath the surface into the gut of the quivering body. The river runs blood red as Rambo, unscathed, climbs ashore to meet his next "patriotic" and violent adventure.

There is a strange attraction to these films. You feel the excitement; you feel like Rambo. You experience his every emotion; your palms sweat and your fists go hard. You want to be like him. You have even thought of joining the Commando Forces after high school. You want to serve your country against the enemy.

When you were younger, you used to read war comics and play with war toys. G.I. Joe and other action figures were your favorites. You took a few lessons in Karate, but you didn't like the teacher or the class because they talked about feelings. The teacher wasn't a patriot or hero like Rambo, anxious to go to battle to defend our country's image. This Karate teacher was soft and gentle. He told you that Karate wasn't for promoting fighting, but rather for learning about how to defend yourself so you don't have to fight. He talked about being peaceful and caring, and you thought he was a wimp. You bought some Martial Arts weapons instead — nun-chucks and a butterfly knife — which you carried until they were taken away by Mr. Nathan one day at school.

BIG SPORT
TV COLOR IV

Suddenly your thoughts are interrupted by your father's voice coming from the front hall. "Hello, I'm home. Hey, anyone here? Come on, let's celebrate!" You can tell he's been drinking again. Your stomach suddenly becomes tight and starts to ache. Your palms sweat as you clench your fists.

"Hey buddy, what's the good word?" your father asks, entering the family room where you are watching TV.

"Nothing," you grunt, not taking your eyes off the TV. You can sense your father's anger and frustration behind you. Your father and you do not get along very well. Sometimes when he drinks, he tries to hit you. When you were little, he did; but now you are too quick. One night last year, on your thirteenth birthday, you and he finally went at it. He was drunk and heard that you had been caught stealing cigarettes from a local store.

"You bum!" he shouted then. "Why can't you be more like your brother Jason? He'd never do anything like that." He swung at you, but you ducked and let him have it. Jason, your mother, and sister had to break it up.

You remember that time now and you think angrily, "If he only knew who taught me how to steal, he'd die." Jason is the biggest thief. He takes his parents' money, liquor, and cigarettes right from under their noses, and they don't ever seem to notice.

You sink down in your chair as your father comes over to you. You are ready for whatever happens. You don't care any more. Sometimes he gets violent, sometimes he spoils you by giving you a bunch of money when he's drunk. You can never tell which way he will go. "Hey, buddy, watching old Rambo. Great, isn't he? Kills all those gooks. Blows them away. They deserve it." He looks at you. "How are you? Get into any fights lately? Hope you stand up for yourself, if you're getting picked on. Here's a little something to get a treat with (as he stuffs a twenty dollar bill into your shirt pocket). Sorry I'm late again. Lots of work to do. This family is very expensive to support!"

You sink even lower in your chair, letting his words and his smelly breath go over your head. Rambo is moving across the jungle to the enemy airstrip. He is trying to get an Attack Hawk Helicopter. You've seen this scene before. He captures the helicopter and flies over the enemy compound shooting rockets into the enemy barracks, bodies flying in all directions, fire and smoke everywhere. You fix your eyes on that flickering screen, hands sweaty, fists clenched, waiting for the big kill.

Chapter 1

WHAT IS A BULLY?

The story you just read took you through one day in the life of a bully. The main character ("you") bullied kids at school, bullied the schoolyard supervisor, and bullied his sister at home. There's no doubt that this person is a bully.

But did you realize that almost everyone in the story was some sort of bully? What about the schoolyard supervisor? Didn't she bully you with commands, threats, ridicule and intimidation? What about the sister? Didn't she bully by making fun of you, teasing you? What about the brother? Wasn't he a bully, but one who got away with it? And what about the father? He's a workaholic who neglects his family, then tries to make it up with tokens of money — and sometimes gets drunk, violent, and bullies his family. The mother is so busy in the business world that she doesn't seem to be there at all.

Bullies are People with Problems

Bullies come in all sizes, shapes, ages and nationalities. They can be rich or poor, educated or ignorant, male or female. Every bully is different, but what they have in common is:

1. They verbally or physically pick on others.
2. They are hurt, angry, afraid, and frustrated.

Because of these feelings and their inability to deal with them, some bullies have done a lot of harm.

Being bullied can have very serious consequences. Some victims of bullies have felt so bad that they have taken their own lives, as happened in the southern United States when a 7th grade student, tired of four years of being called "chubby" and "a walking dictionary," brought a gun to school and fatally shot another student before killing himself. His classmates said, "He was just someone to pick on."

If you have ever been bullied, you know that it doesn't feel good. It's frightening and can be harmful both physically and mentally. That's why I've written this book. I was harmed both physically and mentally due to being bullied as a boy, and I want to help you live your life so that this doesn't happen to you.

> **If you have been bullied,**
> **this book will show you ways**
> **to never be bullied again.**
>
> **If you are a bully,**
> **this book will show you ways**
> **to get what you need without bullying.**

In order to do something about bullying, we have to know what we are dealing with. Let's take a look at the kinds of bullies that exist in the world today.

The Bully Has Many Faces

There are two main kinds of bullies:

1. The Extrovert Bully (Outward)

"Extrovert" bullies are outgoing, aggressive, active and expressive. They want to be on top — in control. They are more interested in things outside themselves than in their own thoughts and feelings. Extrovert bullies are rebels and are usually criticized for their rebelliousness. They often end up in trouble as adults. They are sometimes considered "outlaws."

Generally rough-and-tough, angry, and mean on the surface, they get their way by brute force. But inside, they may feel inferior, insecure and unsure of themselves. They reject rules and regulations and feel a need to rebel in order to achieve a feeling of superiority and security.

2. The Introvert Bully (Inward)

"Introvert" bullies don't want to be recognized. They hide as much as possible. They never rebel; they conform to society. But they also want to be in control. They find other ways to get control — sometimes by smooth-talking, saying the "right" thing at the "right" time, sometimes by misleading, lying, saying and doing whatever they think the other person wants to hear, just to get their way. They deceive people into thinking they mean well. They work on becoming "teacher's pet." They are often so good at bullying, that we don't even notice that they are bullying us.

Introvert bullies get their power through cunning and deception. They seem to go along with the crowd, but because they desperately want to be successful — get the highest, the best, the most — they will lie, cheat, do anything to get what they want.

There are many types of bullies. See if you recognize any of the following. Can you tell if these are introvert bullies or extrovert bullies?

1. **The Super Jock Bully**
   Motto: "I am Number One — yeah, ME!"

2. **The Preppy Bully**
   Motto: "I am the elite of society — the upper crust."

3. **The Movie Star Bully**
   Motto: "Mirror, mirror on the wall,
   I'm the fairest of them all."

4. **The Brain Bully**
   Motto: "I'm smart.
   Therefore I know better than you!"

5. **The Rocker Bully**
   Motto: "Trash it, jam it, freak out! Do your own thing!
   Who cares how it affects anyone else?"

6. The Hippie Bully

Motto: "Tune in, turn on, drop out.
You're a fool to stay straight!"

7. The Patriotic Bully

Motto: "Our country, right or wrong.
Love it or leave it."

8. The Religious Bully

Motto: "There is only one belief worth believing — mine."

9. The Financial Whiz Bully

Motto: "When I speak, Wall Street listens. So you better
listen too."

10. The Prejudiced Bully

Motto: "You are inferior because you are (fill in religion,
race, nationality, color of skin)."

11. The Whining Kid Bully

Motto: (To Parent) "If you don't buy me this, I'll (fill in
your own threat)."

Can you think of other types of bullies? _____

_____

_____

_____ .

There are many different kinds of bullies, but what they have in common is:

1. They are concerned mainly with their own pleasure rather than thinking about anyone else.
2. They want attention, recognition, power, position and fame, and they are willing to use other people in order to get what they want.
3. They want revenge for hurt feelings they have.
4. They do not have the ability to look at the whole picture and, therefore, are not responsible people.

We live in a society in which many people spend their lives looking out only for "Number One." They are self-centered, aggressive, and so focused on "success" that they do not consider anything or anyone else around them. These people create conflict — in their own minds, and in the world.

I know it's difficult sometimes not to be a bully when there are bullies in your home, school, and neighborhood. To make matters worse, many of them bully you around while telling you not to be a bully! But you don't have to be a bully if you decide you don't want to be like them.

What Kind of Bully are You?

In order to stop bullying, the first thing you'll need to do is figure out what kind of bully you are, or how you have been bullied in your life. Pull out a sheet of paper and pen or pencil, and write down. . .

Ways I Have Been Bullied:

1. _____ .

2. _____ .

3. _____ .

4. _____ .

Ways That I Bully Others:

1. _____ .

2. _____ .

3. _____ .

4. _____ .

Here are some questions to help you remember when and how you've been bullied or have been a bully:

1. Have you ever bullied (or been bullied by) a younger brother or sister? If so, give an example.

_____

_____ .

2. Have you bullied (or been bullied by) any of your classmates? If so, give an example.

_____

_____ .

3. Have you bullied (or been bullied by) your parents? If so, in what ways?

_____

_____ .

4. Have you bullied your dog or pet? If so, how?

_____

_____ .

5. Do you fit into any of the bully types described earlier in this book? If so, which ones?

_____

_____ .

6. Have you been bullied by any of the bully types described in this book? If so, which ones?

_____ .

7. Do you think you will continue to be a bully? For how long? Why?

    _____

8. Do you think you will continue to be bullied? For how long? Why?

    _____

9. Do you enjoy being a bully? If so, why?

    _____

10. Do you enjoy being bullied? If not, why not?

    _____

Remember…
In order to learn about ourselves, we must be willing to be honest about our behavior. Being honest, we see ourselves as we are. This means that we do not judge ourselves or others as being "bad" or "good." Feeling bad only creates hatred, guilt and fear. Comparing oneself or another to what is considered good only brings conflict — between who we actually are and who we think we should be. If we look honestly at ourselves *without judgment*, then there will be understanding, learning.

Chapter 2

HOW DOES BULLYING AFFECT US?

When I was a kid growing up just outside of New York City, I was bullied a lot. I am now fifty years old and I still remember how it felt. I sometimes feel the hurt, anger and fear from those incidents that happened many years ago. Almost forty years later, some of the effects of bullying are still with me.

The Day of the Bee Sting
A Story

I remember two bullies in particular: Dickie M. and Vinnie B. I won't mention their last names in case they're still around. (Maybe I'm still nervous that they'll get me now!) It seemed that almost every day one of these two tough boys bullied me. They would make me do things I didn't want to do. They made fun of me, and at times beat me up — just for the fun of it.

I was a big kid who hated to fight, and Dickie knew it. He would get me on the ground, with his knees on my arms, pinning me down. I always felt frustrated and angry and wanted to cry, but I didn't want him to see any of this. I just let him beat me up without doing anything back. No adults ever stopped those beatings, although I wish they had.

One day, Dickie had pinned me down and was beating me up in the neighbor's yard. Without warning, I was stung by a bee in the back. This sudden shock made me jump up fast. Since I was bigger than Dickie, my leaping up threw him across the yard. I was stunned to see him lying there, shaken up.

He looked at me and I looked at him, and we both saw the truth in that moment: *I* was the stronger of the two. From that day on, he never beat me up again, although he did bully me verbally, calling me names and ridiculing me.

His older brother hurt me badly twice, once knocking out my front tooth, and once running into me with his bike on purpose — which threw me into the air, causing me to hit my head on a curb. I had to go to the hospital on both occasions, first to have my tooth and split lip attended to, and second and more seriously, to have my head (near my left temple) sewn up. This hit to the head almost took my life; the doctor said that if the hit had been a little more in the temple area, I would probably be dead. I still feel the effects of that injury.

I Thought There was Something Wrong with Me

I left that tough town in the 8th grade to go on to high school in another nearby town. This new town was very wealthy. I was no longer threatened by physical attacks from Vinnie or Dickie, but I felt threatened in a different way.

In this new town, we were encouraged to aggressively pursue money and power. For the many years I lived there, I was bullied into believing there was something wrong with me for not being money oriented and power hungry — attributes that many in that town thought of as "admirable." I couldn't

compete with these "bullies," so I failed and I felt inadequate for years.

It took me a long time to realize that this was bullying of another kind. While Dickie's bullying was physical, the bullying I got in this new town was mental, or psychological. It wasn't until much later that I realized that mental bullying can be far more dangerous than physical bullying. Strangely enough, it has had a deeper effect on me than getting beaten up.

Bullies in Disguise

As I grew up, I met many types of bullies of all ages, both men and women. Almost everywhere people seemed to be out for themselves: "Me first!" "Go for it!" "Get what you can!" I began to see that bullying didn't stop in high school or college. It was just as apparent in the business world — people competing with each other and bullying to get their way.

Many of these bullies acted like polite gentlemen and women. Many had been educated at some of the best colleges, and they spoke and dressed nicely. How, I wondered, could I feel intimidated by such people? Little by little, I began to see through their fancy outfits, their status-seeking, and their ability to say the right thing at the right time. They're plain old bullies, I said to myself. They're pushing people around just the way Vinnie and Dickie did. But they're using their voices, their clothes, and their positions instead of their fists!

These bullies get what they want by using their minds as a "weapon" to make others afraid of them, instead of using their fists. The best way to deal with these bullies — or any bully — is to know that you can also use your mind instead of your fists, but in a positive way: to keep yourself from being bullied, or from bullying. If you are a bully and don't want to be one, or you have been bullied and don't want to be bullied ever again — you're reading the right book!

Kid Bullies Become Adult Bullies

I noticed, growing up with bullies all around me, that I had turned into a bully myself. I had learned to believe that I needed to be aggressive if I was going to survive in this world.

Even today I sometimes find myself unfairly bullying my wife and daughters, asserting my "power" over them with words or gestures. And at times they do the same to me. At one time or another, we all do it.

Teachers occasionally use their authority to bully. Parents will sometimes aggressively pursue their own needs over the needs of the family. Political and military bullies get power hungry and want to dominate the world. You can be sure, any war we've gotten into was started by bullying.

Kids are not born bullies. We learn how to be bullies from adults. Then we grow up to become adult bullies.

Chapter 3

WHY DO BULLIES AND VICTIMS EXIST?

The Roles We Play

As we grow up, we learn to play various roles in life, such as son, daughter, child, student, team member. Some of these roles change, some stay with us.

Some of these combine to form a life role and lead us to become the adult we grow into. Examples of roles we might become are: teachers, lawyers, doctors, writers, and so on. These are professional or career roles that we take on in order to earn a living or because they are meaningful to us, and we enjoy or have a talent for them.

There are other roles we take on because we care for another person or persons. Some of us get married and have children. We take on the role of husband, wife, mother or father.

These roles that we take on because we *want* to are called <u>conscious</u> roles, meaning that we are *aware* of them. We purposely become an athlete, a policewoman, a nurse, a performer.

There are other roles we take on without purposely choosing them. These are called <u>unconscious</u> roles, meaning that we are *not aware* that we have taken them on. These roles may come from feeling the need to protect ourselves from whatever we feel we need protection from — usually something that has threatened us in competitive activity.

We create these unconscious roles because we are afraid. For example, you may have a fear of taking tests, so you develop the role of "Someone Stupid." You pretend that you are Someone Stupid as a response to the fear that you will flunk your tests. You say, "Of course I won't do well on the test. I'm just so stupid." If you succeed in your role, no one will expect you to do well and you will be safe.

Perhaps you have a fear of playing sports. So, you develop a role of "Someone Weak." You become Someone Weak, saying, "I'm not strong, so you better not pick me for your team." Or, "I better not play this game, because I could hurt myself."

Perhaps you have a fear of speaking in front of the class. In order to avoid doing it, you may create a role of "Someone Shy." You become this character, Someone Shy, and say all the things you think Someone Shy would say.

Fear does this to us. It has a control over us, and can sometimes turn us into "playwrights," writing scripts for ourselves that make us say and do things that we may not really want to say or do.

If you are afraid that people will take advantage of you, perhaps you take on the role of Bully. As Bully, you control other people, telling *them* what to do, so you don't have to do anything anyone else wants *you* to do.

Bully Characteristics

How do you recognize the bullies in your life? Can you tell when you see one? Bully characteristics include...

1. **Facial expressions:** Angry, bossy, frowning — hard, mean, cold, "make my day" scowls.

29

2. **Body expressions:** Signals of power or threat — shaking and/or pounding fists, rude finger displays, hands on hips, arms crossed on chest, legs spread apart, chest out, chin forward, shoulders hunched, swaggering walk.

3. **Language:** Words that are cutting, hurtful, mean or that frighten, harass, embarrass, or tease — like "punk," "jerk," "chicken," "four eyes," "shorty," "nerd," "dork"; attitudes that say, "I'm better than you" or "I deserve more than you."

4. **Behavior:** Isolation; signals of displeasure; violent actions, threats; throwing weight around.

Victim Characteristics

Have you ever considered that a victim (the one who is being picked on) plays a part too? If you've been a victim, think about the role you've played and how you communicated with the bully. Do you think there's anything you did that made you a prime target for a bully to pick on?

You already know that a bully acts like a *superior* person, one who appears to have control and power over another. A victim, on the other hand, acts like an *inferior* person, one who becomes a servant and does what the "superior" person wants. The reason the victim acts this way is because he or she is afraid. The bully and victim take on a "master/slave" or "leader/follower" relationship. They are both afraid, but act out their fears in different ways.

Victim characteristics include:

1. **Facial:** Fearful, timid, shy, fragile, weak, sad, sorrowful.

2. **Body:** Arms limp by side, shoulders drooped, shaking, head bowed, legs trembling, knees knocking, feet turned inward, looking down at ground, crouched.

3. **Language:** Statements like… "I'll give you anything, just don't hit me." "I'll tell my mother on you." "I guess I am a nerd, now can I have my hat back?" An attitude that says, "I feel inferior to you; you are better or stronger than I am."

4. **Behavior:** Quiet, shy; overly careful actions; never pulling attention to him or herself.

The Vicious Circle

A kid may not always get the attention he needs at home. In order to get that attention, he may play the role of "Poor Me." In this way, he bullies his parents into feeling sorry for

him and doing things to make him happy, which gives him a lot of power. He uses "self pity" to manipulate his parents.

Using tears and manipulation in this way, this kid-as-victim turns into kid-as-bully. His parents believe he is weak and needs protection. But actually he's not weak at all. He's very powerful! He uses his feelings to force his parents into treating him as "special" or "overly sensitive."

This manipulation, however, usually backfires. Once he takes on the role of "special" and "overly sensitive," he is often singled out by bullies to pick on. This fits into his role as victim, makes the "Poor Me" all the more real, and makes his parents want to protect him even more.

This is what is called a *vicious circle*. In order to get power in the household, to dominate (and bully) his parents into doing what he wants, the kid pretends (plays out the role of) weak, hurt, fragile, sensitive. This not only gets his parents' attention, which is what he wants, but also gets attention from a bully who picks on the weak and helpless "Poor Me." His parents then protect him even more. Do you see the vicious circle?

If you can see through the roles and games that people play, no one will be able to control you, or get you to do things you don't want to do. You will be able to relate in healthier and more intelligent ways. There is no need for people to bully, control, or rule others. With understanding, human beings can cooperate without control or fear, and share equally in this world.

The Role Models We Have

What makes us start acting out unconscious roles? What influences our thoughts so that we become a character who is not real — an actor with a mask?

A character is defined by his or her:

1. **Characteristics:** Physical attributes and activities. These include how the character looks, walks, talks; what language he/she speaks; the clothes he/she wears.

2. **Influences:** The mental and psychological make-up of the character. This includes how he/she feels, thinks and acts.

We've already looked at the characteristics of bullies and victims. But what influences them? Where do they learn these characters they play? From television? Movies? Performers? Comics? Videos? Books? Parents? Teachers? Community leaders? National leaders?

The things that influence a person to be a bully are the very same things that influence a person to be a victim! Are you surprised? In the movies or on TV, the bully is always portrayed as "the bad guy," the one the "heroes" are trying to bring under control. The so-called "heroes," however, can be just as violent as the "bad guys."

Every bully, at some time in his or her life, has been a victim. If you have been the subject of abuse, there's a good chance you will turn around and dish it out. That's why some of the "heroes" we see are violent. They've been treated with

violence, so they respond with violence. You could say that a bully is a victim in disguise!

Have you ever noticed that when you come out of a theater, you *feel* like, and identify with, one of the characters you've just seen? If the bully is portrayed as a "bad guy," the victim may be portrayed as "the good guy." If the bully is portrayed as "the good guy," the victim can be portrayed as "the bad guy." Sometimes you identify with the "bully" and sometimes you identify with the "victim."

It's easy to identify with a "bully" (like "Dirty Harry") when he's doing away with all the "villains." On the other hand, it's also easy for us to identify with a "victim" (like Woody Allen creates in many of his movies), because we laugh at him, we like him, and we want him to get what he wants.

When we attempt to act out roles we think we *ought* to play, or identify with people we think we *ought* to be, we are imitating "role models" (people to admire and be like). Doing this can cause us to become confused about who we are. Sometimes it's difficult in this world to be who we are — mainly because we've been shown many role models but haven't been taught how to be ourselves!

It takes an incredible amount of energy to work at being like someone else when you're not. Being yourself is the only person you can possibly be and be happy.

Heroes and Heroines

When I grew up, every young man's "hero" was John Wayne in his portrayals of the all-American male — a tough, lonesome, unfeeling, hard, violent, cowboy/soldier. In his movies, agreements were settled by punching, strangling, knifing, or shooting the "enemies." This was the way I was shown how to resolve conflict. The characters created by John Wayne were my role models.

Today, we have very similar "heroes;" we have a wide range of characters on television and in the movies who use more and more violence to solve their problems. Are these characters truly heroes? Do you girls find these characters exciting? Would you like to act like them? Be like them? I have seen women in movies punch, strangle, stab, and shoot people they disagree with, just like men do. They are just as capable of intimidation and control through violence. Who is your female role model?

Talk to your parents and teachers about roles and role models. See if you can discover what else makes bullies and victims play the parts they play.

The World Around Us

Why would a person want to bully you? Why would you want to bully someone? If you can see that there are times when you have wanted to bully, or times when you have actually been a bully, then you know that a bully is not really a "bad" person.

We all get "bully" feelings from time to time. We want other people to do what we want them to do, and we are prepared to use force to get them to act according to our wishes. One reason we feel this way is that we have hurt feelings or angry thoughts — perhaps bad feelings about ourselves. As a result, we try to control someone else, thinking this will ease our pain or protect us from being hurt by that person.

39

We bullies act tough and want to frighten or hurt people who are smaller or "think" smaller than we do. We think other people are better than we are, so we are constantly trying to prove ourselves.

Sometimes we bullies act tough because we're afraid that other people are going to hurt us; we pretend to be tough so other people won't bother us.

Sometimes we bullies act tough because we're upset; perhaps we've been fighting at home with our parents or brothers and sisters. We are so angry inside that we explode and take it out on other people.

Influences Today

There are many different circumstances in your world that could lead you to become a bully. Maybe you've never thought about these before. Here are some possible influences:

A. Your Family

Your family might be the last thing you'd think of as a cause of your being a bully, but your family is at least partly responsible. Here are some ways your family could influence your bullying. Write down any comments you want to make. Do your parents...

1. Offer harsh physical or verbal punishment?

2. Allow you to get away with aggressive behavior?

   _____.

3. Act violently toward you or toward each other?

   _____.

4. Ridicule or hurt you by teasing you or laughing at you?

   _____.

5. Talk much with you?

   _____.

6. Spend much time with you outside of mealtime?

   _____.

7. Take you along anytime, anywhere?

   _____.

8. Praise or encourage you?

   _____.

9. Exchange ideas or thoughts about life with you?

   _____.

10. Set limits on your behavior?

_____ .

11. Know or care where you are after school?

_____ .

12. Care what kind of friends you have?

_____ .

B. Your Friends

If you have an interest in the Martial Arts, for instance, chances are you will make friends with others who share that interest. We generally make friends through what we have in common, to a person we are drawn to, or with someone who wants to be friends with us. In the same way, it's common for one bully type to become friends with another bully type. Gangs of tough youths get together and support one another in their bullying behavior.

We all need to be acknowledged and supported for who we are. When we are rejected by people we know, we feel frustrated and angry. We feel that the world is against us. We get a "me vs. you" or a "we vs. them" feeling.

C. Your School

Your school can contribute to creating bullies without being aware of it. Schoolyard supervisors like Mrs. Potter, in the first story in this book, show kids how to be bullies. Instead of appealing to your *non*violent nature, some teachers express violence and don't understand why some kids are violent in return.

It's important to have rules and regulations that help your school run efficiently. However, if these rules and regulations are overly strict and lacking in understanding, your school may be participating in teaching kids how to be bullies.

D. The Media

All forms of media — television, movies, video games, comics, magazines — can promote violent bully behavior. In the movies, for instance, Rambo is portrayed as a hero; G.I. Joe is a hero in comics. Television, of course, has many bully heroes. When we, as children, see how commonly aggressive behavior is displayed, we learn that it is acceptable, and that in many cases it is rewarded.

Two major hazards:

1. Violent television programs are so commonplace that we become *numb* to the bullying and the violence, and. . .

2. Kids who watch a lot of violent TV programs learn to see the world as a threatening, hostile place, and become *afraid*.

We learn that we must deaden our feelings and become distrusting and aggressive in order to survive.

E. Community Leaders

Some competition can inspire us to improve ourselves, but other forms of competition can be harmful to the way we think and feel. Business can create a very competitive environment. What's the situation in your community? Do business leaders compete with each other and become violent? Or do they "network" and put their know-how together to create a better community?

F. Politicians

We have many fine politicians who work to create changes that are healthy for all of us. Others are politicians because they enjoy being powerful — making decisions, telling people what to do, and how to do it. Because we have political parties, there is often opposition and conflict created between them.

G. Military Leaders

The entire military operation is reliant upon people who give orders and people who take them. Soldiers are bullied into killing and bullied into believing that they ought to kill for their country.

Military leaders of opposing countries play the game of one-upmanship: Which country is better? Who can be stronger? Who can win the war? We are bullied into believing that we ought to want to be better than our friends, stronger than our neighbors, and that we ought to want to win in a struggle with other human beings. I believe we have wars because we have been bullied into believing that we *should* have them.

Influences From Long Ago

We've already learned that parents, schools, communities, and the media can all contribute to teaching us to be bullies. But there is something else deep inside us that can also be a cause.

Have you ever watched a dog and cat when they meet for the first time? Do you remember what they do? They freeze. Then if the cat moves, either the dog chases the cat or the cat stands its ground and fights the dog. This is called "The Fight or Flight Response." The cat either fights the dog or runs away from the dog, or vice versa.

Humans have this response too, to protect ourselves from being attacked. Back in the days of the cave man, humans would frequently be attacked by wild animals. They would have to fight the animal or run away in order to survive. The creature who could fight the best or run the fastest was the one that survived. This phenomenon is called "survival of the fittest." If you have studied Darwin and the theory of evolution, you know all about this.

As far back as man can remember, living creatures have been afraid of predators and have adapted self-defensive, aggressive ways in order to survive and live. Do you think it's possible that today we human creatures try to dominate and control others because we think we still need to in order to survive?

I do. I think mankind learned this behavior long ago, and that we've been passing it down to each other, generation after generation. The question to ask, however, is: Is this behavior necessary today?

When humans lived in small tribes with little food supply and a scarcity of shelters, fighting to survive may have been necessary. But today, with advancements in science and technology, we have created an abundance of food, shelter, and clothing. Do we still have to fight to survive? Why do humans still believe we need to compete in order to live? Why is one person rich and another poor? Why does one country have so much while others have so little? Write down your thoughts and feelings:

_____

_____

_____

_____

_____

Chapter 4

HOW CAN WE STOP BULLYING?

The School of "No Sword"
A Story

There is a story of a famous swordsman, from the school of "no sword" (which means to defeat an enemy without a sword or weapon of any kind). His name was Bokuden and he lived many years ago in Japan.

Bokuden was crossing a lake in a rowboat with a group of people. In the boat with them was a tough looking and arrogant Samurai (a type of warrior/soldier) who boasted about how good he was with a sword.

"I am the greatest swordsman," claimed this strong warrior. "Nobody can beat me." The passengers eagerly listened to this braggart's endless stories about winning many fights. But Bokuden took no notice and was dozing as if nothing were going on about him. This made the Samurai very angry. He came up to Bokuden and shook him saying, "Hey, aren't you listening? Come on! You also carry a pair of swords. Why aren't you joining in on the conversation?"

Bokuden responded quietly, "My way is different from yours; it consists not in defeating others, but in not being defeated." This just made the warrior angrier.

"What is your school then?" asked the warrior.

"Mine is known as the school of 'no sword'," Bokuden responded calmly.

"Why then do you carry a sword?" cried the Samurai.

"To protect myself from wild animals, not to hurt people."

The braggart became very frustrated, and he shouted, "Do you really mean that you can fight with no sword? Can you fight me with no sword?"

"Why not?" answered Bokuden calmly. The warrior called out to the boatman to row to the nearest island. Bokuden suggested that it would be better to go to the island farthest away because the nearer island had people who might be attracted to the fight and might get hurt. The Samurai agreed. The boat headed for the island farther away.

As soon as they came near enough, the Samurai jumped off the boat and drew his sword ready for combat. Bokuden slowly took off his swords and handed them to the boatman. He was about to leave the boat to follow the Samurai onto the island when Bokuden suddenly took the long oar from the boatman and, pushing it against the land, gave a hard backstroke to the boat. The boat moved away from the island and out to the sea, leaving the enraged Samurai standing on the shore in combat position.

When the boat was safely away from the island so the warrior couldn't follow, Bokuden said, smiling, "This is my school of 'no sword'."

In this book I want to show you the way to put an end to bullying. For those of you who have been bullied, you will be happy to know that you don't have to be a victim. For those of you who bully others, you may be happy to know that you no longer need to bully people to get what you need in this life. I know this will be a challenge for you. Are you ready?

The First Three Steps

The way to stop bullying is to:

1. Take an interest in stopping it.
2. Learn to understand why people bully.
3. Develop nonviolent skills to deal with bullies.

Take an Interest in Stopping It

If you truly want to put an end to bullying, the first thing you need is a genuine interest in stopping it. This interest is not something I can give you. It can only come from you. I have it because I was badly bullied. Perhaps you have been bullied and you wish you could do something. You can! Maybe knowing that you can will give you an interest.

Perhaps you've been bullied, and you aren't even aware of it. If you've ever felt that you would like to "get back" at someone, there's a good chance that you have been bullied. If you don't like that feeling of being out of control, you may wish there was a way to put *you* in charge. There is! Knowing that there is a way may give you an interest.

Learn to Understand Why People Bully

The second thing you need is an awareness of how bullies act and a desire to understand why they act that way. When you understand why the bully acts in a certain way, you are less likely to want to "get back" at the bully and more likely to work out a way to bring you and the bully to some level of agreement. At the very least, you will understand the bully's needs and learn what you must do to protect yourself. If you are a bully, once you understand why you are one, you will see ways you may be able to change and still get what you want.

Who do you fight with? Your brothers or sisters? Your parents? Your classmates at school? In order to *not* fight, it's important to look at reasons why we do fight.

Here are some reasons why other young people fight. Are they similar to yours?

- Someone makes fun of you.
- Someone embarrasses you.
- Somebody wants something you have.
- You want something somebody else has.
- You feel empty or hurt and want to hurt back.
- Somebody wants to control you, or make you do something *they* want you to do.
- You have a need to control someone, or make them do something *you* want them to do.
- You are jealous of someone.
- Someone is jealous of you.
- Someone wants to be better than you.
- You want to be better than someone you know.
- You are hanging out with the "wrong" crowd.
- Someone wants to prove how tough he/she is.

What other reasons can you can think of?

_____ .

_____ .

_____ .

Once you understand why another person wants to fight with you or why you want to fight with them, you can think about fighting before you actually fight. You can *stop* yourself from reacting out of fear and *think* about what you can do to prevent a fight from ever taking place. Talk about control! That really takes a lot! But it can be done!

Develop Nonviolent Skills
to Deal with Bullies

Along with an interest in learning how to stop bullying, and an understanding of why bullies bully, the third thing you need is to develop nonviolent skills to deal with bullies. Are you ready to learn some? They are really fun.

Winning by Losing

There are ways to win that do not involve fighting. Bokuden proved this with his school of "no sword." He won by *not* fighting. Bokuden was a master warrior because he knew how to win by not hurting others or getting hurt himself. This takes know-how and practice.

When you've been confronted by bullies, you may have spent a lot of time trying to figure out ways to fight — to get back. What I'm saying is just the opposite. Once you've learned alternative nonviolent skills, you will have the confidence and know-how *not* to fight.

You've probably been threatened with a fight at one time or another. Perhaps you've had to fight or run away to avoid getting beaten up. Maybe you've discovered that neither fighting nor running away is a good way to solve conflict, and both can hurt you — physically or mentally.

Let's look at what it means to have the confidence not to fight. It's actually very simple. If a bully picks on you, and you don't know how to defend yourself, what happens? Do you take a stand and fight back? Do you run away? If you do one of these things, you're not alone. Most people do, because they are afraid and don't know another way.

When you are afraid, however, what happens is that you "freeze up." This tensing of your body and mind does not help you; as a matter of fact, it can contribute to your getting hurt.

There are two types of skills you need to handle a bully's attack:

1. Physical self-defense skills.
2. Nonviolent alternatives.

We are going to talk about these skills in more depth in the pages that follow. The more you learn about these skills and alternatives, the more exciting it gets. You begin to find out that you can have control in situations that have threatened you in the past.

If you knew you had the skills to protect yourself from any attack by a bully, wouldn't you feel less afraid and more confident? Being less afraid, you wouldn't freeze up, right? And being less afraid, you wouldn't need to fight back, right? Nor would you have to run away!

Chapter 5

HOW VICTIMS CAN BECOME WINNERS

Do You Mind If I Warm Up?
A Story

A big kid had been picking on a younger boy for months. The younger boy had tried many ways to get out of fighting, which worked well for a time. But this older tough kid kept on. Nothing seemed to stop him. Now he was coming down the street again, after the younger boy.

"Hey you, punk. What makes you think you're so hot?" the big kid shouted. The younger boy had nowhere to go since his way was blocked by an apartment building and one long dark alley.

The big kid stood tall and close to the younger and shorter boy. "So I finally got you away from your friends! I'm going to pulverize you, squirt, because you wouldn't give me your lunch money."

The young boy stood calmly and looked the older youth straight in his eyes. "I see that you intend to fight me. I've tried everything to not fight, so I guess now I'm going to have to fight you. But before we start, do you mind if I warm up?"

The bully agreed and the young boy began punching, kicking and striking the air with great speed and power. It was obvious to the bully that this youth knew how to defend himself. Upon seeing the skill of the younger boy, the bully made a lame excuse and a rapid retreat.

This is a true story of a famous Karate teacher when he was a young boy. It goes to show that victims can be winners and that there is great strength in the way of nonviolence.

Karate Gives Confidence

One way to learn how to defend yourself and achieve the confidence *not* to fight is to learn a physical self-defense technique like Karate. Karate teaches you how to block, punch, kick, and strike. It is important for you to keep in mind that Karate teaches these skills to *protect* you, to help you feel secure in your ability to protect yourself. Knowing these skills keeps you from being afraid when a bully picks on you. Rather than "tense up," you "center" yourself and prepare to protect yourself. You feel so confident knowing these skills that your "attacker" is often intimidated before you ever use them! You use your mind instead of your fists!

**Karate should be learned from a qualified
and intelligent Martial Arts teacher.
It cannot be learned properly from a book.**

**If you decide to learn
physical self-defense techniques,
take the time to find a qualified instructor —
someone who teaches physical skills
and the nonviolent mental skills
that go with them.**

I am a Karate teacher who has taught for over 30 years. I teach a style of Karate called Take Nami Do. This style of Karate shows a young person like yourself how to have the confidence *not* to fight. At the same time, it teaches students how to get out of a threatening situation by nonviolent means. What we do really works! I have taught hundreds of young people how to solve conflict nonviolently.

The important thing to remember is that a student must be taught *both physical and mental skills* of self-defense. The physical skills give you the confidence that you could handle a fight if it ever came to that. The mental skills offer you ways to resolve a fight before the fighting ever begins.

Using Your Head

You may be able to think of ways to peacefully avoid fighting other than those that follow, but here are twelve ways kids have used that definitely work.

Making Friends. One of the easiest ways to stop a fight from happening is to be friendly and kind to the bully. Most bullies feel hurt or angry, and being friendly may help them feel better. If they think you are treating them with respect, they may offer you respect too. But be careful! Bullies aren't used to being treated with kindness, so they may not respond well at first.

Using Humor. Sometimes you can stop a fight by being funny, or telling a joke. But be careful! The bully might think that you are making fun of him or her. Make sure the bully knows that the joke or story is not meant to be at his or her expense.

Trickery. Trickery means that you fool the bully by pretending. Remember the swordsman from the school of "no sword"? He left the bragging Samurai on a far island by himself. He used trickery. Other ways to trick a bully include:

- Pretending to be sick.
- Feigning poison oak or ivy (depending on where you live).
- Speaking in a foreign language (that you make up).
- Telling the bully you just had an operation.
- Saying your mother or father is about to pick you up.
- Telling the bully that your father, mother, brother or sister is a member of the police, or a Karate instructor.

Can you think of others? Trickery is a good way to stop a fight because it makes the bully think of something else and takes the bully's mind off hurting you. Again, be careful how you do this. The idea is to *prevent* a fight.

Walking Away. You may be angry and frustrated and feel you have a right to stand up for yourself and fight back when someone has been bullying you. But does fighting back solve anything? All it does is hurt people. When you fight back, you become like the bully, using violence as a way to solve the problem. Walking away may seem like a difficult thing to do. But just think — you haven't been hurt, and you haven't hurt anyone else. It takes a lot of strength to simply turn your back and walk away.

Agreeing with the Bully. Many fights start when a person feels insulted. If someone calls you a name or tries to embarrass you, instead of responding with anger or fighting, just stop. Wait and watch what happens inside of you. What do you see? Do you feel angry or hot inside? Do you feel like punching or slapping the one who insulted you? If your answer is yes, it's important to try something new:

1. *Just watch* these feelings inside you.
2. Watch them come up and watch them go. Don't react!
3. Don't do anything about them. Just let them be there.

After you feel calm again, agree with the bully. For example, if the bully calls you "Shorty" and accuses you of being afraid to fight, tell him or her that this is true — that you *are* short and that you *don't* like to fight. Agreeing doesn't mean that you are not as good as someone who is taller than you, or that you are a coward because you don't want to fight. These are facts and nothing to be ashamed of.

If what the bully says is untrue, then you can *disagree* and gently tell the bully that what he or she just said is simply not true. Or you can walk away and avoid the bully's insults. The bully wants to get you angry so you will fight, but if you don't react to the insult, you are like bamboo in a strong wind: you bend but you don't break; you straighten up, unhurt. *And* you prevent a fight.

If you go through something like this, talk about it with a friend, your parents or a teacher. Experiences like this can be frightening. It feels good to have someone listen to what you've been through and comfort you.

Refusing to Fight. A fight takes two people. If you refuse to fight, this can stop the bully from hurting you. You may feel angry and afraid. You may want to run away or cry. You may feel you have to stand there and get beaten up because your friends are watching and they'll think you're scared if you run away. But turning your back, walking away, refusing to fight are all alternatives that take great strength. And they are all better than fighting.

Standing Up to a Bully. Standing up to a bully means that you tell him or her with words, with your body, with how you present yourself, that you do not want to be bullied. You can say something direct, like, "I know you don't like me, but I'm not going to let you hurt me!"

You may think that this would make a bully want to fight with you even more. It might! But many times standing up to bullies surprises them. They are expecting you to be afraid, and when you're not, they back down. It can depend on what else is happening at the moment. If there are other kids standing around watching, standing up to the bully may just make him or her want to fight you even more. But if you are alone with the bully, it just may work.

Remember:
Standing up means that inside yourself
you have decided you are not going to tolerate
being bullied any longer.

Standing up to a bully is an important decision. Once you make it, you will find the courage to use alternatives.

Screaming/Yelling (Kiai). The human voice is very powerful. Singing is a good example. Singing can make you feel sad, happy or full of energy, even angry. So using your voice is a very good alternative. You can scream, "NO! I WON'T LET YOU HURT ME!" or you can yell, "HELP!" or "FIRE!" You may think it's silly to yell "Fire!" but this will cause people to act very quickly and come to see what is happening. (Do this only when absolutely necessary.)

You can also use "Kiai," pronounced key-ah. "Kiai" in Karate is a strong yell that is used with a block, punch, kick, or strike. It gives power to a self-defense technique because it causes the stomach muscles to tighten, adding strength. But "Kiai" also scares a bully and for a fleeting moment they forget wanting to fight you, and you can get away before anything further happens.

Ignoring. This is an alternative that requires caution. When you ignore the bully, you pretend that he or she is not there. This may work well with some bullies, and it may backfire with others. You have to practice to find out. Sometimes you may want to use more than one alternative at a time; combining strategies can be more powerful than using one alone. Ignoring is an alternative you may want to use in combination with walking away, or trickery.

Using Authority. There are two ways you can use authority to demonstrate your power...

1. Show the bully that you are not afraid and you will not allow him or her to hurt you. Here you are being your own authority, using your own power.

2. Call someone else to help you who is more powerful than the bully. Powerful doesn't always mean having physical strength. It can also mean someone who is older and *in* power, like a parent, teacher or police person.

You may think that calling an adult who is in power is "ratting" and being a coward. But this is not true. If you have tried to stop the bully by one or more of these alternatives and the bully keeps on trying to hurt you, you have a right to get someone older who has authority over young people to help you. That is what parents, teachers, police, or playground supervisors are there for. If you do this, perhaps you will avoid getting the beatings that I got as a kid when there were never any adults around.

Kids *and* adults need to stop bullies. No one has the right to bully anyone! Hopefully the person you have called upon to help will be wise enough to settle the fight in a gentle and intelligent way. There are adults and kids who have been specially trained to do this. Is anyone trained to handle arguments and fights on the playground at your school? Whether anyone else is trained or not, you will benefit from learning skills that will help you end conflict before anyone gets hurt.

Reasoning, or Talking It Out. Some kids just know how to speak well. They've learned to use words to convince other people of what they want or don't want. For the rest of us, learning to reason or talk it out requires practice. Perhaps your parents or teachers can help you learn this skill. It's very important to know how to reason, to think out what to say and do, so that you don't hurt others and they don't hurt you.

As you grow into adulthood, it becomes more and more important for you to know how to reason — to think clearly and intelligently. As you grow up, you take on more responsibilities and have more details to work out. If you start now, you will have an easier time of it later. You will have had lots of opportunities to practice reasoning skills!

Taking a Karate Stance (or warming up). Hopefully you will have tried *everything* you could to stop a fight before you take a Karate stance. This alternative should be used *last* because it means using your physical body in a way that shows the bully you are strong, you know how to protect yourself, and you are prepared to defend yourself. Taking this stance does not mean you are going to fight; it means you are ready to, if necessary. You hope, by taking this stance, that the bully will back down and leave you alone.

If there are kids around watching, keep in mind that with an audience the bully might feel he or she is now forced to fight or will lose face. So be careful how and when you use this alternative.

Now that you know some new alternatives, you will be able to try them out for yourself. To use them, you will need confidence. And you will gain confidence by using them. This confidence is your real power. You will feel happier, more in control of your life, and your friends will see that you are stronger for *not* fighting.

There are many other ways to stop conflict before it starts without resorting to violent, physical means. We have just mentioned a few. Get together with friends or family and talk about the variety of nonviolent alternatives that are available.

> **Remember:**
> **A bully has *no* right to hurt you.**

Practice Makes Perfect

When you learn nonviolent alternatives, you are better able to defend yourself. You already know that the reason you want to be able to defend yourself is to have the confidence to *not* fight.

Confidence comes from *practicing* these nonviolent alternatives to fighting. They are skills, like playing an instrument or participating in a sport. The way to do them well is to do them often. Anyone who is interested can learn them, but it takes training and practice.

Just as a singer or keyboard player knows several songs and plays each one for a different effect or occasion, every situation in which you use a nonviolent alternative has a different mood. Each moment is new and needs to be looked at freshly; an alternative that works in one situation may not work in another. Having alternatives in the back of your mind, ready to use, can help you avoid being bullied.

Sometimes a bully does not respond to your efforts and may need the professional help of a counselor. If you suspect this is the case, *get help*. It's always okay to get help when you need it. If you're afraid the bully might want to "get back at you," ask an adult to get involved without letting the bully know you're the one who asked for his or her help.

In the sections that follow, you will find practice situations that can help you deal with bullies. Practice these over and over so you are prepared to act in a real situation if one should ever come up. In addition to preparing you for real life circumstances, the exercises are really fun.

Roleplaying: A Way to Understand

In order to help you experience this feeling of confidence, I have created some roleplaying samples for you to try. If you are a bully, it's important to experience what it feels like to be a kid being picked on. And if you've been a victim, it's important to "get into the shoes" of a bully so that you can understand his or her feelings.

Have you ever roleplayed? Roleplaying is just like what it says: it's playing a role or part, as if you are in a play. In the roleplay situations that follow, you will get a chance to make use of the nonviolent alternatives you learned in the previous section.

In each roleplay situation, play the victim, AND play the bully. It doesn't matter which you play first, as long as you have the opportunity to play BOTH. This way you have a chance to see the situation from *all* sides. You can perform the roleplays with friends, parents or teachers.

These roleplays also include the bully and the victim's "alter egos." (The alter ego consists of inner thoughts and feelings — what we feel inside but don't show outside.) These unspoken feelings may help you understand why the bully and the victim feel the way they do.

The cast of characters for the first roleplay: The Bully, the Victim, and Mr. Wood.

The Bully can read the Bully Alter Ego part as an "aside" (under his or her breath). The Victim can also read the Victim Alter Ego part, but it should not be directed to the Bully — only to the audience, or as an "aside." The lines that are in *italics* are not to be read. *They are describing your role or are actions to be taken by the actors.* If you have trouble understanding this, ask for help.

Remember:

1. Really get into your part.
2. Act out the alter ego parts.
3. Ask for help if you need it.

Roleplay #1

Bully: *(Alter Ego)* "Boy, it looks like she has a lot of money. Look at her nice clothes. I wish I had her money. Her parents must really love her."

Bully: "Give me your lunch money!"

Victim: *(Deny/Trickery)* "I don't have any money; I bring my lunch from home."

Victim: *(Alter Ego)* "This is scary. I feel safer because I've practiced how to handle myself when I'm threatened. What was it my

70

teacher told me about getting out of this type of situation without fighting?" *Takes a deep breath and feels the scared feelings.*

Bully: *Reaches out and grabs victim.* "I don't believe you!"

Victim: *(Trickery)* "Be careful, I've got poison oak!"

Bully: "I still want your money!"

Victim: *(Authority — Calls Teacher)* "Mr. Wood! I need some help."

Mr. Wood: *(To Bully)* "Do you need money? I'll be glad to loan some to you for now. I can also help you find ways to earn money if you need it so badly."

Bully: "Yeah, I do need money bad. My family is in trouble. I'll pay you back by working, I promise, or maybe you can find me a job somewhere."

Questions:

1. How did it feel to bully the Victim?

   _____ .

2. How did it feel to use trickery?

   _____ .

3. If you were the Bully, what happened when you heard about the "poison oak"?

   _____ .

71

4. If you were the Victim, how did you feel about calling in an "authority" figure?

_____

_____ .

Roleplay #2

Bully: "Hey Brain, give me your homework!"

Bully: (Alter Ego) "This kid always gets the teacher's attention because he knows all the answers, so the teacher likes him. He must be good. Schoolwork is hard for me; I don't like it when the teacher calls on me and I don't know the answers. I wish I could please the teacher, but I must be dumb. I never get the teacher's attention 'cause I'm bad."

Victim: (Making Friends and Talking It Out) "I'd like to help you, but I already turned it in this morning."

Victim: (Alter Ego) "Oh, no! Him again. How do I get rid of this guy?"

Bully: "You always get good grades so you're going to do my homework from now on, or else you're in big trouble."

Victim: "I can't do your homework for you because that isn't honest, but I've got a better idea."

Bully: "Yeah, what's that, Brain?"

Victim: "I'll make you a deal. I'll help you with your homework, if you do something for me."

Bully: "Like what?"

Victim: "Let's meet after school today and talk about it. Maybe we can help each other. I hear you're really good at basketball and I'm lousy at it. Maybe you can teach me something."

Questions:

1. If you were the Victim, how did you feel when the Bully demanded your homework?

   _____

   _____.

2. If you were the Bully, what did you think you would gain from getting the Victim to do your homework?

   _____

   _____.

3. As the Victim, how did you feel offering to help the Bully and getting the focus away from you?

   _____

   _____.

4. As the Bully, were you surprised that the Victim thought you could be helpful? Why? Why not?

   _____

   _____.

Roleplay #3

Bully: "Hey, you stupid punk — you sat in my bus seat. If you do it again, I'll break your face!"

Bully: *(Alter Ego)* "This guy looks easy to beat. Now it's my turn to win. I'm always getting it at home and the big kids at school beat me up. I'm ticked! I feel like busting! I feel like hurting someone else, for a change."

Victim: *(Agreeing)* "Sorry. I guess I was stupid all right. Here's your seat."

Victim: *(Alter Ego)* "Wow! This guy could hurt me. I wish I could run away, but that just makes me feel lousy."

Bully: "What did you take my place for then, punk, huh?"

Victim: "I didn't know it was your seat."

Bully: "Everyone knows this is my seat."

Victim: *(Trying to Make Friends)* "I'm new at the school, and I don't know my way around yet. Maybe you can help me."

Bully: "I don't help punks! I think you need a lesson in good manners." *Makes a threatening gesture.*

Victim: *(Using Humor and Trickery)* "Wait! Before you hit me, I want to let you know that if you beat me up my sister will be upset because she likes you. She told me that she wanted to go out on a date with you. She likes kissing boys."

Bully: "Yuk! Girls are goofy and I ain't going to let no girl kiss me! Hey, are you joking? That's a laugh. What a clown!"

Questions:

1. As the Bully, did you feel good getting the Victim out of "your" seat?

   _____

   _____ .

2. As the Victim, how did you feel when you decided not to run away, but to talk to the Bully?

   _____

   _____ .

3. As the Bully, were you surprised to have the Victim ask you for help? What did this do to your "tough exterior"?

   _____

   _____ .

4. As the Victim, were you scared using humor? Could you tell how the Bully was going to react?

   _____

   _____ .

These situations are made up. But they are based on real occurrences. If they are not realistic to your particular situation, you can create your own roleplaying scenes.

If you invent your own roleplaying situations that work for you, I would like to hear about them. My address is at the back of the book. If you send them to me, I will pass them on to other young people. In this way, you'll be helping others.

In order for all of this to work for you, you must practice. Your mind is a source of power, but you need to exercise it the way an athlete exercises his or her body. If it's going to be ready to use when necessary, it has to be in good shape.

> **To cope with bullies of any kind,
> use the power of your mind.**

Chapter 6

HOW BULLIES CAN BECOME WINNERS

Have you ever felt:

Anxious?	Helpless?
Worthless?	Powerless?
Out of control?	Unfairly punished?
Ridiculed?	Harassed?
Hurt?	Vengeful?
Ashamed?	Angry?
Humiliated?	Frustrated?
Insecure?	Lonely?
Enraged?	Unloved?
Rejected?	Violent?
Ambitious?	Greedy?
Pressured to conform?	Pressured to compete?
Scared?	Afraid of not "making it"?

Afraid of not living up to the expectations of others?

In other words, have you ever felt that everybody is picking on you?

Well, if you have had these feelings, then guess what? You have felt like a victim *and* you have felt like a bully! The desperate feelings listed above are feelings shared by both bullies and victims. The painful thought of "What did I do to deserve this?" is a thought that has entered the minds of both the bully and the victim the bully picks on!

What happens, then, is a vicious circle: The bully who picks on someone also feels like a victim — someone who has been picked on.

Bullying is a "Lose/Lose" Situation

We all want what we want. This is neither good nor bad; it's just a fact. The problem begins when we try to *push* another person into doing what we want. This is bullying.

We might believe that if everybody thought and acted the way we do, the world would be a better place. We can think this as much as we want; there's no right or wrong about it. The problem comes, however, when we try to *force* another person into thinking and acting the way we do. This is bullying.

Have you ever bullied someone? I have. At times throughout my life, I've tried to get people to do things by pushing them and intimidating them. This is called a "win/ lose" situation. Somebody wins and somebody loses.

If you have bullied someone in a situation like this, you may already know that it's a losing game. You may have the strength to bully someone and make them do what you want but, in the end, you're not getting what you really want. That person may do what you want for the moment, but once you leave, he or she will go back to being whoever they are. What you really need — real caring and affection — you don't get. It's really a "lose/lose" situation: your victim loses self-esteem, and you lose self-respect.

We all feel hurt, anger, hatred and malice at times. It's not an easy world that we live in. It's okay to *feel* that you would like to hurt someone, but it is *not* okay to actually do it. As human beings, with clear thinking minds and respect for one another's humanity, we have the responsibility to not hurt each other and to deal with our thoughts and feelings in nonviolent ways. Unfortunately, sometimes we step over the line and someone does get hurt. We are not perfect. The most important thing to remember is — to *try,* each time, to nonviolently deal with your anger towards another. Even though you may slip and hurt someone, if your intention is there to *not* hurt, perhaps the next time you will be more alert and sensitive.

Roleplaying: For Bullies Only

Here are some roleplaying exercises for acting out peaceful ways to win. If you're not used to being peaceful, these exercises may feel strange at first. But I know you will get the hang of them with a little practice.

Here's how to do it. Read the part of the Bully as well as the part of the Bully's Alter Ego (the Bully's thoughts and feelings). The lines in *italics* should not be read; the Bully should *act these out.*

Remember:

1. Really get into the part.
2. *Act out* the Alter Ego (what you think and feel).
3. Stop! And think!
4. Ask for help if you need it.
5. Use the script to think up your own roleplays.

Roleplay #1

Bully: *(Alter Ego #1)* "Boy, I really feel like letting this kid have it. He's acting like a crybaby." *Bully gets ready to punch the kid.*

STOP! THINK!

Bully: *(Alter Ego #2)* "Yeah, but what good will it do to hit this mama's boy? He's just trying to get sympathy." *Bully unclenches his fist.*

Bully: "Why are you acting like such a wimp? You're just feeling sorry for yourself."

Questions:

1. How did it feel to get angry with the kid?

2. How did it feel to almost punch him?

3. How did it feel to let the fist go?

4. How did it feel to talk to the kid?

Roleplay #2

Bully: *(Alter Ego #1)* "I know she's better off than me. Look at those neat clothes and that super car her parents drive. I feel like giving her a hard time. She's always showing off."

STOP! THINK!

Bully: *(Alter Ego #2)* "Yeah, but who cares, anyhow? I don't really like that type of dress. Maybe someday I'll earn enough money to have fine clothes. Why waste my time on this? I've got better things to do. She does look great, though."

Bully: "Hi, Sarah. I like what you're wearing. You look great."

Questions:

1. How did it feel to get angry with Sarah?

2. How did it feel to want to give her a hard time?

3. How did it feel to let go of your hostile feeling?

4. How did it feel to give Sarah a compliment?

_____ .

Roleplay #3

Bully: *(Alter Ego #1)* "I know he bumped into me on purpose. I'll show him!" *Bully gets ready to punch the other person.*

STOP! THINK!

Bully: *(Alter Ego #2)* "He apologized, said it was an accident. Look at the look on his face. He's afraid of me." *Bully relaxes.*

Bully: "Okay. I accept your apology. Accidents happen. Just be more careful next time."

Questions:

1. How did it feel to get bumped into?

_____ .

2. What memories came to mind when you got bumped?

_____ .

3. Did the apology sound sincere?

_____ .

4. What did the fear on his face tell you?

_____ .

5. How did it feel to accept his apology?

_____ .

Roleplay #4

Bully: _(Alter Ego #1)_ "What a stuck-up kid she is. Won't even look at me. Thinks she's too good for me."

STOP! THINK!

Bully: _(Alter Ego #2)_ "Okay, she's stuck-up. Why should I let that get to me? _I'm_ okay. I don't need to walk around with my nose in the air."

Bully: "You know, I think you've got a problem. How come you're so stuck on yourself? You know, you could have more friends if you weren't so conceited."

Questions:

1. How did you get the thought that she was "too good" for you?

_____

_____ .

2. How did it make you feel to think of her as "stuck-up"?

_____

_____ .

3. What made you take your focus off of her and to see yourself as "okay"?

_____

_____ .

4. How did it feel to tell her that *she* has a problem?

_____

_____ .

5. Do you want to be friends with her?

_____

_____ .

Roleplay #5

Bully: *(Alter Ego #1)* "What a nerd. Look at that jerk's jacket. Full of inky pens and scraps of paper. What a brain. Maybe I'll knock his squeaky bike over."

STOP! THINK!

Bully: *(Alter Ego #2)* "Hey, he could help me with my math. He's a real whiz at it."

Bully: "Listen, maybe you could do me a favor. Maybe I could do you one in return? I'm good at working on bikes; you're good at algebra. Maybe we could trade."

Questions:

1. How did it feel to want to push the kid around — put him down and knock over his bike?

   _____

   _____ .

2. What happened inside you when you stopped and thought?

   _____

   _____ .

3. How did you feel when you remembered he's got a sharp brain for math, your weakest subject?

   _____

   _____ .

4. How did it feel to express an interest in working *with* him instead of pushing him around?

   _____

   _____ .

Roleplay #6

Bully: *(Alter Ego #1)* "What a weakling. She can't even do one chin-up!"

STOP! THINK!

Bully: *(Alter Ego #2)* "I guess that's not her thing. I wouldn't want to be that skinny, but I guess that's her business."

Bully: "Hey, bones! Just kidding. Need help with your training? Let me give you a couple of tips. Honest! Come over here and I'll show you how to be Superwoman in no time. I'm serious! There's hope for those bony biceps!"

Questions:

1. How did it feel to want to call her a weakling?

_____ .

2. What thought went through your head when you went from putting her down to sympathizing with her?

_____ .

3. How did it feel to kid her?

_____ .

4. How did it feel to offer her help?

_____ .

5. How did it feel to make the situation humorous?

_____

_____ .

These are a few examples of what can run through your head and what you can do to change your negative thinking to positive thinking. The point to remember is that although you may *think* and *feel* like bullying someone, you don't have to. You have the power to turn your thinking around. Sometimes doing it takes more strength than bullying.

There are times when we *all* feel hurt, and times when we *all* want to strike out. But if we STOP and THINK, we can find peaceful ways to behave and still get what we want.

Talking Things Over

If you feel angry, talk to someone. Tell them how you feel. It's okay to feel! No matter what the feeling is! If your brain is full of revengeful thoughts, share them with a trusted friend. Sometimes just talking can help relieve the tension created by hurtful or fearful thoughts and feelings.

There are people around who care and want to help you. You are not bad or wrong. But you may need to make some change so you can feel better. It may seem tough at first, but you *can* do it! Millions of people who grow up in terrible situations and become bullies learn how to grow out of it. They understand that the way *out* of it is a new way *into* their own minds — a different way of looking at things and a real desire to change.

What you need to change your behavior:

1. **Interest** in wanting to change.
2. **Energy** that inspires a feeling of wanting to act.
3. **Commitment** to carry it through.
4. **Awareness** of what is happening.
5. **Skills** that provide the ability to change.
6. **Alternatives** for acting differently.

Do you have these qualifications? If you are a bully, or if you are someone who has been bullied, you can change and do things that will help you. Here are a few suggestions:

1. Talk to your parents about what you feel.
2. Request a family time when you can all share your lives together.
3. Think and talk about ways you can get what you want without hurting other people.
4. Practice these ways.
5. Appreciate who you are and praise yourself for doing things you feel proud of.
6. Instead of teasing your friends and family, help them.
7. Communicate in ways that make you feel good and make others feel happy.
8. Find friends that support the positive sides of yourself.
9. Watch healthy, nonviolent television programs.
10. Play video games that make you feel creative and peaceful. Many of them are even more exciting and challenging than the violent ones.
11. Be selective in choosing movies to see.

12. Read books, magazines and comics that make you think, laugh, or cry. There are thousands that are interesting and fun, that make you feel cooperative instead of aggressive.
13. Create activities that include, and make, friends.
14. Learn how to speak in a way that promotes understanding and cooperation.
15. Find ways to build up your confidence so that you don't have to fight (out of fear) to defend yourself or to get what you want.
16. Realize that fighting is not a healthy means of getting what you want.
17. Get help if you need it from a qualified professional (teacher, counselor, school administrator or psychologist). If you broke your leg, you would go to a doctor for help, wouldn't you? It's the same thing. No matter how strong we are, sometimes we simply need help.

> **You *can* change!**
> **You just have to *want* to.**
> **It's up to you,**
> **with a little help from your friends!**

Chapter 7

AWARENESS IS EVERYTHING

The Meaning of Success

Do you know what a "pecking order" is? The phrase is derived from the lifestyle of chickens. When the toughest chickens are asserting their authority over the weaker ones, they actually peck them into submission.

We humans have our own means of establishing a pecking order — from the subtle violence of kids using verbal threats, to one nation challenging another.

Do you see people in your school or neighborhood working to become "successful"? What does being successful mean to you?

1. Getting the friends you want?
2. Having a CD player, fashionable clothes, state-of-the-art equipment?
3. Being healthy?
4. Being a loving, caring person?
5. Getting along with other people?
6. Contributing to world peace?

We learn the meaning of "success" from adults. They learned about "success" from adults when they were children, and now we learn it from them. There are different meanings for "success." For some people, it's having millions of dollars; for others, it's living a healthy life.

Many people associate success with winning, being right, or getting to the top. In order to achieve this kind of success, people sometimes:

1. Compete with others in conflicting ways.
2. Say one thing and do another.

Competition that is friendly and cooperative doesn't hurt anyone. However, competition that is hostile can hurt everyone. We can also be hurt by people who say one thing and do another. These people are called hypocrites. For example, someone who says, "Be gentle, cooperate," and whose actions are hostile and competitive, is a hypocrite.

Our world today is hypocritical. It says, "Don't be a bully; it's not nice; it's not good." But many people are bullies and earn money, power and honor for the bullying they do.

There are some lawyers who dress in expensive suits and advise their clients to lie: "Say what I tell you to say, and we'll get you off easy."

There are some doctors who wouldn't take some of the pills they prescribe, but they say: "Take this medicine. It may have a few minor side effects, but it'll kill the pain."

There are some real estate brokers who try to sell a home they know has problems. They insist: "You'd be crazy not to grab this house."

We don't need destructive competition in the world today; we need cooperation. If we truly want cooperation, we need to stop *being* bullies, we need to learn how to deal *nonviolently* with bullies, and we need to take a hard look at how we are living our lives. We can make a good living financially and live sane and healthy lives without being bullies — and wind up healthier and happier!

Being *aware* of our human pecking order is the first step in not getting caught up in it. There are many creative, exciting and rewarding careers and ways to be in this world without becoming a bully or getting involved in a pecking order. Talk about these with your family and friends. This could be a good topic of discussion at one of your family or school "talk times."

It is generally accepted in the world today that violence, competition, attaining success, dominance and power are "good" things, heroic ideals. When you came into this world, this view was already well in place. Therefore, you may have come to accept this as normal and natural — but that doesn't mean it is.

Although you live in a competitive, violent society, you do not have to live *your* life that way. What you think and feel represents who you are. Your thoughts and feelings are reflected in your actions. If you have "positive" thoughts and feelings, you will act in a positive way. If you have "negative" thoughts and feelings, you will act in a negative way. How you think and feel and, therefore, how you act depends on *you* and your attitude.

You Are What You Remember

In school, you learn "subject matter" information such as math, history and geography. Your brain remembers that 10 x 8 = 80, and that Columbus discovered America in 1492.

In addition to that kind of information, your brain remembers "thought and feeling" information, such as painful and pleasurable events. If, for example, you broke your brother's bike and were punished harshly for it (perhaps your parents told you that you were "bad" or "no good"), memories of that incident are stored away in your brain, along with other images from other past incidents.

As you go through life and experience hurt, your brain stores these memories. This accumulation of past experiences of hurt, anger and frustration contribute to "negative attitudes," which are part of who you are. Have you heard people say that you are what you eat? Well, in this case, you are what you remember.

Sometimes our minds play tricks on us. We think to ourselves:

"I feel hurt, so I must deserve being hurt."
"I *feel* bad, so I must *be* bad."

If you've ever thought this way, you are not alone. All of us have past experiences that cause us to have negative beliefs about ourselves. Here is a story from my own life:

When I was young like you and in school, I had an image of myself as being stupid — and it hurt. Because I wasn't a "good" student and getting high grades, my friends and teachers had an image of me as a "bad" student, and not very smart. In high school, the college counselor even told me that I would never get into college. I began to believe in this opinion others had of me. This negative image became a belief and affected how I saw myself and the world; I believed that I was bad because others told me so. Slowly, I began to replace this negative information I had stored from the past with new information from my own observations and experiences of myself. And, by the way, I went on to college and received a Doctorate Degree in Psychology, and also *taught* at college! See what can happen when you free yourself from negative thinking!

Can you think of anything that happened to you in the past that causes you to think negatively about yourself today? What is it?

Turning Negative Thoughts Into Positive Thoughts

If yesterday's experiences of pain dwell in your mind, these experiences will affect the way you relate to other people today. Here's something you can do about it. When you find yourself thinking negative thoughts about yourself:

1. **Recognize** that these "negative" thoughts and feelings are happening in you.

2. **Just allow** the "negative" or "bad" thoughts and feelings to be there. Don't judge them. Don't do anything about them. Just let them be there — and look at them.

3. **Talk** about your negative thoughts and feelings with someone you trust. It's important to pick someone, even if you feel scared about trusting anyone.

4. Look at these thoughts and feelings and notice that they have to do with the past and need not interfere with who you are now.

5. Focus on the things in your life that are good, instead of on past hurts. Start with one good thought; then let others come into your mind.

6. Substitute truthful, positive thoughts and feelings about yourself and your special talents. Everyone has something to offer. Think about it. What's your special something?

Life doesn't judge you. You do! Life doesn't hold on to what hurt you yesterday. Your mind does! Life is new and fresh every moment. Your thoughts are old and from the past!

> **The wonderful thing about living is that life is always forgiving.**

Knowing this, *you* can be responsible for who you are *now*. You can be the person you want to be *now*. The only thing holding you back is you!

Remember:
1. Understand negative thinking.
2. See your real gifts.
3. Think helpful thoughts.
4. Live in this period of time called *now*.
5. See the world as fresh and new.

I know there is a person you want to be that may be a little different from the person you are now. Know that the person you are now is good and worth being. The following, however, are thoughts to help you become even more of the person you want to be. Say to yourself:

1. I belong by contributing.
2. I can make intelligent decisions and am responsible for my own behavior.
3. I am interested in cooperating.
4. I can decide to *not* fight.
5. I can find acceptable, healthy ways to get what I need without bullying.
6. I can find positive ways to express my emotions.

Say these over and over again and you will see changes begin.

Chapter 8

HOW BULLYING AFFECTS WORLD PEACE

The Difference Between Heaven and Hell
A Story

A young armed arrogant warrior came to see the old wise man.

"Oh wise man, tell me the secret of life. What is the difference between Heaven and Hell?"

The wise man thought for a moment and said, "You are a stupid young fool. How can an idiot like you even begin to understand this? You are far too ignorant."

On hearing these words, the young warrior became enraged. "I could kill you for what you said." He started to draw his sword to kill the wise man when the wise man said, "*That* is Hell!"

On hearing these words, the warrior put back his sword. "That," spoke the wise man, "is Heaven!"

Have you ever read about people like Joseph Stalin, Adolph Hitler, Attila the Hun, Genghis Khan, or other world political and military leaders? These people were horrible bullies! They violently gained power over others because they wanted people to believe in and live the way of life they thought best. They tortured and killed millions of people for their ideals.

These people are extreme cases, but there were *millions* of others who contributed to their terrible aggressions. All the officers, soldiers and politicians who supported and served these leaders were also bullies. Our world has been run by bullies for thousands of years.

We have enjoyed very little peace on earth or time when humans have been able to cooperate nonviolently. The issue of peace has been of great concern to all sensitive human beings since the beginning of mankind.

Propaganda: Verbal Bullying

The kind of bullying that happens on the school playground is essentially the same bullying that causes international wars — both use physical force or hostile aggression to "win." Behind this physical aggression is a mental aggression — it is verbal bullying, and it's called *propaganda*.

People use propaganda to win people over to their way of thinking, usually by telling lies or exaggerating. Propaganda has been used for centuries to "brainwash" or condition people into believing all sorts of things.

When you watch television, the propaganda you see most often is in commercials — advertising meant to bully you into buying products. By using light, pictures, sounds, music, and images, advertisers persuade you to buy the products you see on the screen. Did you know that the average young person watches between 30,000 to 40,000 commercials a year? That's a lot of propaganda!

Propaganda is also used to create wars. Countries use the media (TV, radio, newspapers, political cartoons, videos, film, magazines and even comics) to bully you into believing that their way is "the right way." Every nation uses propaganda to get you to believe that "the other side" is bad, evil — "the enemy." For decades, until the historic improvement in relations between the two countries, Americans had been taught to see Russians as brutal and warlike. Russians had been taught to see Americans as money-grubbing, cunning and untrustworthy. How do you suppose that image was created?

Why do countries do this? To get you to fight? To defend your nation? To defend your way of life? Like a bully on a playground, propaganda *pushes* you to act.

Nationalists (people devoted only to the interest of *their* nation) can brainwash you into believing that in order to live you must take sides, align yourself with their particular belief system. This becomes the basis of *destructive* competition and creates war, great pain and sorrow in the world. If we divide ourselves from other people, then we are creating the conditions for conflict and war. Therefore, we must understand why and how we become divided, why there are separate groups, political parties, religions, nations. This doesn't mean that we all have to look alike or speak the same language. Differences can be beautiful, and give the world variety. But belief systems and propaganda produce differences that lead to division, conflict and destruction. People who use propaganda are bullies.

Following are the two final sections of this book. One is called "Activities" and includes exercises that can help you develop nonviolent alternatives and improve your understanding of the bully/victim relationship. The last section, "Questions to Help You Stop and Think," provides a list of questions for you to ponder. You may want to look them over alone, or discuss them with others at school or at home.

However you use these activities and questions, I hope you will continue your search for ways to create a world in which cooperation is the number one priority.

Bullying, as you may now see, has world-wide implications. If we can understand how and why we bully each other at home or at school, we can begin to understand how and why nations also bully, leading to conflict and war. For, as I see it, it is one and the same. What do you see?

Karate at Work
A Story

Jeff was in his woodshop class at school, working on his project. In came Chris, the school bully.

"Hey, hot shot, hear you've been taking Karate. What for? Are ya' Bruce Lee or something? Come on, Kung Fu fool, show me your stuff. I want to see *your* Karate!"

Jeff kept on quietly and carefully sanding his project. He looked up slowly, then straight into the eyes of Chris, and said with a friendly and confident smile, as he kept on sanding, "I'm doing it now."

Chapter 9

ACTIVITIES

Understanding Aggression

You may have heard your parents, teachers or counselors use the word "aggressive." I have used it in this book. Do you know exactly what it means? Actually, it has two meanings:

1. **Aggressive: "energetic or full of energy"**

   Example: "Mark is an aggressive promoter of healthy lunches for kids."

   (This kind of aggressive behavior is generally not harmful.)

2. **Aggressive: "harmful action against another, usually a verbal or physical attack"**

   Example: "Beth can get pretty aggressive if you don't give her what she wants."

Sometimes it's fun to fool around — perhaps wrestling, pretending to box, or doing Karate kicks. But there are times when fun turns to anger and people get hurt. Some adults think that fighting is natural. They say, "Boys will be boys." Or, "Some aggression is perfectly natural." Both boys and girls fight. But *is* it natural to fight?

The following are activities designed to help you learn about aggression so that no one gets hurt. You can do them with your friends, or at school with the assistance of your teachers. These activities are not only fun, they also help you to learn about yourself.

Activity #1: Shoving

Select a partner. Face one another, about two feet apart. Raise your hands to shoulder level. Reach out and place your palms on your partner's palms. Keeping your hands at shoulder level, push against the other's hands. Push as hard as you can. See if you can push your partner back. (Take care not to slap each other's hands or hurt one another in any way. Pushing becomes more of a game or a challenge than a fight.)

Activity #2: Inner Scream

Find a comfortable place to sit. Close your eyes and imagine that you are going to some quiet, faraway place by yourself. Think of someone that bothers you (perhaps someone who bullies you). Imagine that there is no one for miles around. Continue to think of the person that irritates you. Let him/her bother you even more. More! More!

Now, silently scream. Open your mouth and scream silently, as loud as you can! Be aware that you are alone; no one can hear you.

Now think of the person who bothers you again. See yourself doing something that would stop him/her from bothering you. Be aware of how you can, in your mind, stop that person from bullying you. Open your eyes and discuss what you felt.

107

Activity #3: Getting It Off Your Chest

Sit in a circle. Each person gets to tell another something that is bothering him/her. For example, "Mike, you really bother me when you make fun of my wearing glasses. I feel like punching you when you do that." Or, "Janice, I feel angry when you try to be the teacher's pet and tell on others. I feel like getting you into trouble so you will get suspended from school."

The rule is to let the person "get it off his or her chest." Don't defend yourself. When someone addresses you directly, just listen to what he or she has to say about you. You too will have your turn to say what bugs you.

Now, each person should think about what others have said to them. It is important to consider whether it is true or not. Some things you can change, others you may not feel you need to change. What are you willing to change? Share that with the person who addressed you. For example, "John, I was just kidding about your glasses. I didn't know that my joking bothered you so much. Sorry, I won't do it again."

This activity allows you and your friends or classmates to get the things that bug you off your chests without harming anyone.

Activity #4: The Laughing Bully

Can humor be aggressive? Can a person bully another by saying something funny about that person?

Have you ever used humor to hurt someone? Have you felt hurt when someone made fun of you? Can people be cruel when being funny? When you make a joke about someone,

what are you doing? Can people hide their anger in humor?
How else might you express your anger rather than through
joking?

Be aware of when you use humor throughout the day (or
week) to express feelings you have about another. Watch for
times when you use it to hide anger. Also, be aware of how
others use it to hide their anger.

Discuss these questions with your friends or classmates.
What did you find out about humor?

Activity #5: Ruler for a Day

Each person takes a turn at being "The Ruler." The Ruler
gets the others to "serve" him or her. The "servants" have to do
what The Ruler asks them to do. Some examples of being
served might be: to have the group carry you around, or bow
down to you, or do errands for you, or get you food and drinks.
Your wish is their command.

Remember that it is a game! Nothing can be done that
will hurt another person. Each person gets a turn. After, sit
down and talk about how you felt — being The Ruler, and
being the servant. This game or activity allows you the
opportunity to get what you want without force or bullying,
and it's fun.

A New Role to Play

"I can't back down."
Have you ever had that feeling?
"I've got to save face."
Has that thought run through your mind?

109

If you are a bully or if you are a victim, you may feel you have a reputation to uphold and, in the eyes of the world (friends, teachers, parents), you can't back down. As a bully, you fear being seen as a chicken, or coward. As a victim, you fear the same thing.

What if I told you that there is a way you can back down and feel good about it? Well, it's true. There is. If your image of yourself is that of a Rambo, a tough guy who nobody would dare mess around with, then you cannot back down. If your image of yourself is Poor Me, and you feel you have to save face or the other kids will think you're a coward, then you cannot back down.

If, however, your image of yourself is that of a *peacemaker*, then your action to "back down" is right in line with this self-image! A peacemaker does not fight. A peacemaker makes peace.

Seeing Yourself as Peacemaker

A famous Karate teacher once said:
To subdue the enemy without fighting is the highest skill."
— Gichin Funakoshi

Is it in your self-image to be a peacemaker? Do you think you could get recognition and praise for being a peacemaker? A peacemaker is not a wimp; when you decide to be a peacemaker, you show yourself and others that you have the power and self-control to solve conflict nonviolently — without fighting. This takes far *greater* strength than fighting. To me, this is the highest art.

What characteristics and skills does a person need to have to be a peacemaker? To be a peacemaker, you must:

1. Understand what creates conflict.
2. Develop skills to resolve conflict nonviolently.
3. Visualize yourself being a peacemaker.

I have talked about what causes conflict (what creates a bully and what creates a victim), and I have offered roleplaying skills so you can begin practicing resolving conflict peacefully.

Now, all you have to do is take the third step — *see* yourself as a peacemaker! This is called *visualization,* which means to create a picture in your brain of what you want to happen or who you want to be.

Let's try it. Find a quiet, undisturbed place where you can sit comfortably. Lying down can make you sleepy, so sit in a comfortable but firm chair. Close your eyes. (You can do this alone, with me guiding you, or a trusted friend can assist you.)

Peacemaker Primeval

1. **See yourself in a deep jungle.** The time is two million B.C. You are in very primitive times. Suddenly, two animal-like monster cave men come crashing out of the jungle and confront each other. They grunt, beat their chests and make threatening looks and gestures.

2. **You notice the monster cave men are small.** Either they are small or you are quite big. They look like little

kids and you look like a large grownup. You see that they cannot hurt you.

3. **You speak to the cave men**. "Listen," you say. "Are there ways you can solve your conflict without fighting?" You sit down between them and start talking to them as if they are children you have great affection for.

4. **"You are the first humans," you tell them.** "So why are you acting like wild beasts? You are greater than wild beasts: You can think and reason. Let's put our heads together and think up some intelligent, peaceful ways to solve your problem. If you learn how to stop fighting now, maybe this will have an effect on the whole history of mankind."

This is just one fun, imaginary example of seeing yourself as a peacemaker. You and your friends, parents and teachers can make up your own scenes. It really doesn't matter what they are as long as you actually see yourself becoming a peacemaker. Other possible scenes could include:

1. A football game in front of an applauding audience.
2. A boxing match in front of a rowdy audience.
3. An ancient Greek coliseum where gladiators are about to fight each other.

Peacemaker as Star

See yourself on a school playground. Two make-believe kids are about to fight, and you are a famous athletic, movie or rock star whom these kids really admire. Get a good, clear image of yourself as this favorite positive hero. (Who did you choose to be?)

As they are about to start fighting, they see you coming. Their mouths drop open. Their fists drop as they look in awe at you approaching. The group of kids around these two also see you coming.

"Wow! Look who's here! I can't believe my eyes. It's (fill in the name of yourself as a peaceful hero)."

When you are amongst them, you say, "Look. There must be a way to get along. Why not try to work your problem out peacefully. Instead of wanting to hurt each other, use that energy to think of ways you can cooperate. Come on, let's work together!"

Everyone cheers as you pat the two kids on the back. Then everyone, including the two would-be fighters, ask for your autograph.

This is a simple, pretend situation. It gives you a chance to see yourself as peacemaker in your fantasy.

Now, here's one a little closer to home...

Playground Peacemaker

See yourself on *your* playground. Remember an incident, or make one up, between two real people that almost led to a fight. See yourself as a *real* peacemaker, helping to work things out nonviolently. See your teachers, parents, even the two fighters, thanking you for what you did.

Do this slowly, watching and doing as much as you can in detail. Take your time. You may want to practice this over and over. Then you may want to set up some pretend situations with a friend or two in which you play the peacemaker role. After you see yourself as peacemaker, practice helping the would-be fighters (in your skit) to learn nonviolent alternatives to conflict.

Hopefully this will be just one more way in which you can creatively and peacefully deal with bullying. I'm sure that you can do it. If you really want to, you can succeed.

Ways to Relieve the Effects of Bullying on the Body

It takes a lot of energy to control other people. As you grow up, this need to control can cause great damage to your well-being. You are affected physically and mentally by the stress of dominating others.

When you are young, your mind/body has the flexibility of youth. You are generally healthy and can recover from illness more quickly than can an older person. So perhaps you don't yet see the effects of constant stress on you. But certain physical disturbances begin to appear, such as:

1. Extra weight.
2. Nervousness.
3. Illness.
4. Exhaustion.
5. Anxiety.

114

Stress will eventually wear down your body and mind, and serious illness can occur. The mental and physical effects of being aggressive, pushy and controlling can hurt or even kill you. Remember there can be *very* serious consequences to bullying. But you *can* do something to help yourself or someone you know. Please get help! We all need it sometimes.

To Relieve the Stress

There are many ways, some presented in this book, that can reduce and even end bullying — if a person *wants* to. There are also some activities you can do to help relieve the stress of bullying or being bullied. You can:

1. Take a long walk or run.
2. Play with a pet.
3. Swim.
4. Dance.
5. Practice the Martial Arts (with the proper teacher).
6. Do gymnastics.
7. Lift weights.
8. Sing or play a musical instrument.
9. Write down your feelings.
10. Talk to a friend.

Can you think of other things to do to relieve stress?

_____

_____

_____

Manners

"Manners" is an old-fashioned word that means acting politely. In the school where I teach, manners are a very important part of what we do. When you learn the form of Karate that I teach, manners show you how to act in accepted ways. Rather than thinking of manners as something we do for a reward, or to avoid being punished, we look upon them as a pleasant way to get what we need. Without manners there would be disorder.

Thinking of manners as skills to learn can be fun — a lot more fun than thinking of them as something you "have to" do. They help you to get along with others and to get what you want without offending anyone. Here are some examples:

Unhelpful Ways:	Helpful Ways:
"Gimme that!"	"May I please have that?"
"Shut up!"	"Would you please keep your voice down?"
"You're wrong!"	"I don't see it that way."

On a piece of paper, list some other unhelpful and helpful ways you can express yourself. You can even make a game out of it. One person can say something in an unhelpful way, and another person can respond saying the same thing using manners.

Manners are simple and so effective. They are taught to you because someone cares enough to want you to speak and

act in ways that will help you get along in this world. Try the helpful ways and see if you do, in fact, get along better in your relationships. You might be surprised.

In Karate, we bow out of respect for the teacher and for each other (student to student). Bowing is a form of manners in the Martial Arts.

One day I asked my young students to try something at home that night. I asked them to bow every time their parents asked them to do something, and then to do what they asked. At the next class, the students shared what happened.

One student said, "My mother asked me to clear the table of dishes after dinner, so I bowed and said yes, and did it without any complaint. My mother almost fell over, she was so surprised!"

Chapter 10

QUESTIONS TO HELP YOU STOP
AND THINK

*"Be patient towards all that which is unsolved in your heart, and try to
love the questions themselves."*
— Rainer Maria Rilke

I want to leave you with some questions to think about.
Questioning is *very* important in your education. Questioning
makes your mind sharp and intelligent. It's a form of exercise;
just as physical exercise keeps your body in shape, questioning
keeps your mind in shape. When you *stop, think* and *question,*
you are more likely to be who you are and less likely to react in
harmful, conditioned ways.

Here are some questions that can help you think over and
discuss what you have just read in this book.

1. Do you believe that "might is right"?

   _____ .

2. If so, who taught you this?

   _____ .

3. What influence does the media have on you as far as
   bullying is concerned?

   _____ .

4. Who are your heroes?

   _____ .

5. Are they really heroes, or could they be villains in disguise?

   _____ .

6. Do you believe in harsh punishment for children who disobey?

   _____ .

7. If you do, why?

   _____ .

8. Do you think young people bully because they feel hurt?

   _____ .

9. Do you think bullies act that way for the fun of it?

   _____ .

10. If you think so, why?

   _____ .

11. Do you believe that "boys will be boys" and that it's okay to be tough and push people around?

_____ .

12. Do you feel the pressure to conform?

_____ .

13. Do you feel the pressure to compete?

_____ .

14. Do you feel the pressure to be an "A" student?

_____ .

15. To be a super athlete?

_____ .

16. To get into the best college?

_____ .

17. Do you think trying to be "perfect" (good) is harmful — a form of bullying oneself?

_____ .

18. What "types" of bullies can you think of?

_____ .

19. What are the effects of bullying individually?

_____ .

20. What are the effects of bullying globally?

_____ .

21. Do you think that a victim can cause bullying in some ways?

_____ .

22. Are only boys bullies?

_____ .

23. What are the differences between male and female bullies?

_____ .

24. What makes you want to fight: For the fun of it? Being called a coward? To save face? Standing up for yourself? A special cause? Your country?

_____ .

25. Do you think bullying creates "the enemy"? How?

_____ .

26. Do you believe fighting solves problems?

_____ .

27. Can violence bring about peace?

_____ .

28. What can you do to create more peace: In your home? In your school? In your community? In the world?

_____ .

29. Do you see yourself as a "peacemaker"? If not, why not?

_____ .

30. Do you really care about changing?

_____ .

31. Do you really care about helping others to change?

_____ .

32. Are you willing to get help if you need it?

   _____ .

33. Isn't it really up to you?

   _____ .

A SPECIAL NOTE TO THE YOUNG READER

I hope that you have enjoyed my book and have learned what you can do about being a bully or a victim. The most important thing to remember is that we don't need to bully. We do so because we are hurt and afraid. Each of us feels alone, separated from each other in our own world, our own life. It is important to see that we are not alone, that we are all human beings who need to cooperate for our *mutual* survival. Many people feel that they must fight for their *own* survival because they feel isolated. So being a bully is a part of *self*-preservation; bullies think they need to compete, to be aggressive and push to get what they want. This way of living creates pain and suffering. And in the extreme, war.

What we need is so simple. What we need is to care for each other. And in order to care, it helps to understand what makes a bully so you can be free of being one yourself or of being a victim of a bully. If we can understand why people bully, then there can be real peace in the world because we will have understood one of the major causes of war. Understanding is intelligence, and being intelligent is caring, loving.

If you want to share your thoughts or feelings about anything in this book, please feel free to write to me. I enjoy hearing from people who have read my books. It makes me feel cared about, which is such a wonderful feeling.

With care,

Terrence Webster-Doyle

Terrence Webster-Doyle

Atrium Society, P.O. Box 816, Middlebury, Vermont 05753

A Personal Message to Adults Who Live or Work with Young People

My father used to say, "Boys will be boys." I don't think he meant anything negative by it — just that, in his eyes, boys fighting and being rough was just the way it was. Boys were allowed, and even expected, to be somewhat aggressive and combative. This was, and still is to some extent, the accepted, conditioned view. But as a boy I suffered a great deal from this attitude because I was not particularly aggressive — that is, "manly." I did not like fighting with my male friends or being aggressive with girls, as many of the other boys were. I felt pressure to be aggressive and to dominate, yet I couldn't live up to this expectation. So I got picked on, bullied. And it hurt, both physically and emotionally.

I still feel hurt, late into my adult life. And I know it has its roots in my childhood. I grew up just outside of New York City in a somewhat tough town. Back in the 1940s and 1950s there were gangs, really tough and violent groups of young men who fought each other. If you weren't in a gang, you were considered a "punk." Coming from a more educated family, I presented myself to others in an "ungang-like" fashion, which also added to my getting picked on. White buck shoes (Do you remember Pat Boone's popular shoes of that era?) were in fashion, but *only* among the few preppy-looking kids whose parents insisted that they wear them. My white shoes lasted one day. They were stepped on, scuffed, kicked and trampled in a matter of hours. I realized that in order to survive, I had to "do as the Romans do!" So I joined a gang. I gave up my father's image of a young Madison Avenue junior executive wearing natty Ivy League clothing, and donned a nylon kelly green jacket, dark green pegged pants with saddle stitching, and engineer boots with a fake brass buckle. My gang was called the "Crusaders." Our jacket had a buccaneer-like character on the back, sword in hand, making a bold, threatening gesture to those who dared to look.

My gang days were short-lived. Not only did I shock my family by the seriousness of the situation (which it was), but the cartoon "Crusader Rabbit" suddenly became popular, which made our gang look ridiculous!

126

My sister saved me by convincing my parents to move to the next town, a rather conservative, very preppy (now called "Yuppie") town. There I could redon my white buck shoes, madras shirts, and fit right in with everyone else.

But there was a serious side to all of this that has lasted with me. There was a great deal of fear and anguish in being picked on for being different, for not being aggressive, or "manly" enough. I remember, and still feel deeply, the fear and humiliation I felt when I was bullied. Two bullies in particular were relentless in their attacks on me. I used to try to sneak home from school to avoid them, which just made it worse because they saw that I was afraid. I felt so helpless and desperate. I couldn't talk to my father because I felt that I would not be a "man" in his eyes if I showed weakness by not standing up to these bullies. So I finally joined them and became their lackey, their victim and whipping boy. It was only by moving away from them that I could stop this humiliating relationship, but unfortunately it carried over. Other young men sensed and took advantage of this "weakness." But their bullying was of a different nature and was "acceptable," encouraged and honored by society.

In this town, being aggressive wasn't the same as in the "tough" town. It wasn't gross or uncouth, like it was with the gangs. That was low class, crude. This type of bullying was an educated, refined type that would eventually allow you entrance to prestigious East Coast universities and later to prestigious New York law firms, or brokerage houses. This was a type of aggression that was expected of a "winner," to be a "success," and was held in high regard. This was the upper class version of the conditioned mentality that "boys will be boys." The traditional three-piece suit replaced the gang outfit, the yachting or country club insignia replaced the crusading buccaneer on the imitation silk jacket. This type of bullying governed the minds, hearts, and souls of the elite young men who desired to be Number One, to join the ranks of the rich and powerful, the ruling class. So I went, as the saying goes, from the frying pan into the fire. I changed my costume again and proceeded to take my position in the pecking order, on a more insidious totem pole. The pressures were tremendous and pervasive.

In my former town, at least the adults around us disapproved of our aggression and gang behavior. They wanted us to act like gentlemen. But in this new situation, teachers, parents, school administrators, counselors — indeed, it seemed, the whole town — approved of this form of "gentlemen's" aggression. "Boys will be boys" meant that a young man had license to be aggressive, superior, even violent. It was a part of the "old boy's network." You would be allowed to join the club if you went along with the tradition. But, again, I couldn't give in — not entirely.

I became a preppy rebel. At times, I wore the costume of the rich, East Coast spoiled kid. At other times, I was decked out in my James Dean "rebel without a cause" outfit — red poplin jacket, collar defiantly turned up, worn blue jeans, and the infamous engineer boots with the fake brass buckle. I would vacillate between going to fancy formal dances in a tuxedo, to slouching around town with a Marlboro cigarette dangling in a cool fashion from my sneering, rebellious mouth — looking as if I was one of the wild ones, which I was in some tragicomic sense. I was only fourteen years old and had no real understanding of what I was doing. I was a Doctor Jekyll and Mister Hyde character, wavering between total conformity and absolute rebellion. On the one hand, I desperately wanted to be accepted as "one of the elite," and on the other hand, I wanted nothing to do with them because I could *never* live up to their expectations. And neither could they, nor can anyone.

The tremendous pressure, the struggle between conformity and rebellion took its toll on me. I was a drunk, a failure, and felt sick most of my teenage years — both physically and mentally. I was torn apart by my conflictive roles. My teachers subtly or overtly pressured me to "get good grades" to "be acceptable," or "go to the right college," to "get the right job." And even in church — where I thought there would be some compassion, some sense of decency and kindness and love — I subtly and overtly got the message "be good!" which translated into "conform!" It seemed that church and state were not separate, but were together in their combined effort to condition young people to be "successful."

It was this "success" that I found to be the most insidious bully! It was this "success" that I so rebelled against! And it is the pressure for "success" that creates such tremendous conflict in the world —

individually and socially! Although it has a comic side, it is very tragic.
This "boys will be boys," aggressive, success syndrome has caused great
suffering for many individuals over many years. It is even a direct cause
of war, that extreme outcome of militarized aggression to be Number One,
the elite, the best. The schoolyard bully and the national military or
political despot are similar in their orientation. And conversely, the
schoolyard victim can become cannon fodder for generals in their
relentless need to conquer and control. Or, the victim turns bully in
revenge. And today it is no longer, "boys will be boys," because girls have
joined the ranks. Many girls are no longer satisfied with growing up to
raise the warriors; they too want to join in the battle. They have learned
from men how to be cold, cunning and aggressive. The femininity and
compassion of women are qualities that are rapidly fading and being
replaced with a macho mentality, a "go for it" yuppie ambitious tenacity.

My story is not so unusual. The effects of bullying touch us all. Most
human beings have suffered from being picked on and many have grown
into adulthood with a chip on their shoulder, taking their frustrations out
on the less strong, the less aggressive, those beneath them in the pecking
order. As adults, we need to take bullying very seriously. Bullying can
have disastrous consequences!

According to an international study published by the National Safety
Council, entitled School Bullying and Victimization (NSSC Resource
Paper), "...15 percent of school children are involved in bully-victim
problems. One in 10 students is regularly harassed or attacked by
bullies.... Those who had been childhood bullies tended to have children
who were bullies. These men were also found to be abusive with their
wives, punish their children severely and have more convictions for
violent crimes...." Bullying is considered a major problem in Japan and in
Scandinavian countries where violence, vandalism and general
delinquency are increasing. This violence is one reason why the Japanese
Prime Minister has called for major educational reforms.

In Japan, cases of suicide have resulted from being bullied, as well as
situations where victims have murdered their tormentors. In Tokyo, a
special "bully buster" force of 30 officers arrested more than 900
youngsters for bullying in a 6 month period. And this is just the tip of the

iceberg. Bullying is an international problem that has prompted experts from around the world, in the fields of education, sociology, psychology, criminal justice, and juvenile delinquency prevention, to meet and discuss the problem and possible solutions. Findings show that young people are pressured to passively conform and, at the same time, to aggressively succeed, which creates tremendous stress on them and their families. In essence, bullying is a learned way of life that reflects our socially accepted, often violent, self-centered way of living.

Why do we teach our children to be bullies, to be "successful" in this way? What do we gain by this? Can we see the devastating effects of this unnecessary, aggressive way of life? Individually and globally? It seems that schools generally teach our children to compete, and our conventional religious institutions aggressively pressure them to be "good," and to display acceptable behavior.

Acceptable behavior in this society is a double-edged sword. On the one hand, we are told to be successful, compete, gain, "go for it!" While on the other hand, we are expected to be kind, considerate, good. This double bind pressure divides us and creates conflict, inwardly and outwardly. And should you really succeed, as in business, then the same people who encouraged you to be successful now want to tear you down, to make you fail. Everyone loves the underdog. But let the underdog succeed and the other edge of the sword cuts deeply. It's as if we are in a perpetual struggle: "Succeed, but don't be a success." "Compete, but be considerate of others." "Be aggressive, but be kind."

I am not trying to be negative, vindictive or cynical. I want to point out *actual behavior* so we can come into direct contact with it, to understand it as it is. It seems to me that we have not been able to deal directly with this behavior because we have been judged by others and, in turn, judge ourselves. Judgment, and the effort to conform to idealistic, "moral" behavior, trying to be what we are not, creates great conflict. Judgment creates pain and prevents us from looking at the *fact* of our behavior. We start out by judging others, bullying them to meet our needs, and then end up bullying ourselves in order to keep up with our self-projected ideas.

What the essence of this book is saying is that we are all subjected to, and are engaging in, one form of bullying or another. We all have been raised in an incredibly violent "dog eat dog," cutthroat world. Even the way we approach solving these problems can become another form of bullying and, hence, produces more conflict. The only "solution" (which is really not a solution as in "problem solving") is to: 1) come into direct nonjudgmental contact with the fact of what we actually are, and 2) begin to be aware of the deeper causes of this reactive way of living. If we can observe the tendency of bullying in ourselves as it is happening and question its place in our lives, then our deeply conditioned tendency can end in that moment of clarity and questioning. It is the nature of a question to hold the conditioned impulse in a state of abeyance. The tendency may come back a moment later, because of the tenacity of conditioning, but if one is alert, sensitive, questioning and challenging conditioning, then the tendency can end — each time one is aware of it as it happens.

Being aware of this deep conditioning to bully, to manipulate, to be self-centeredly aggressive, can only come about in society if enough of us become seriously concerned about understanding this issue. Teachers and parents together need to assist each other in understanding this tendency in themselves, and help their children to be aware of conditioning as it occurs. Bullying is not a moral issue, nor is it an intellectual problem to be solved. If we can begin to create programs directed at understanding this issue of bullying, then we will help raise a generation of young people who will have the possibility of being free of its devastating effects. And as we begin to explore bullying, we will come to realize the deeper, underlying causes of many of the problems of humankind — the social strife and sorrow created by humans divided in themselves and separated from each other in a nonsensical, violent pursuit for self-survival. Survival in the 21st Century means survival for all, a global cooperation that must go beyond defensive, fearful, individual, self-centered, aggressive tendencies.

ABOUT THE PUBLISHER

Atrium Society concerns itself with fundamental issues which prevent understanding and cooperation in human affairs. Starting with the fact that our minds are conditioned by our origin of birth, our education and our experiences, the intent of the Atrium Society is to bring this issue of conditioning to the forefront of our awareness. Observation of the fact of conditioning — becoming directly aware of the movement of thought and action — brings us face-to-face with the actuality of ourselves. Seeing who we actually are, not merely what we think we are, reveals the potential for a transformation of our ways of being and relating.

If you would like more information, please write or call us. We enjoy hearing from people who read our books and we appreciate your comments.

Atrium Society
P.O. Box 816
Middlebury, Vermont 05753
Tel: (802) 388-0922
Fax: (802) 388-1027
For book order information:
(800) 848-6021

ABOUT THE ARTIST

Rod Cameron was born in 1948 in Chicago, Illinois, but has lived in Southern California most of his life. He studied painting with the "Dick and Jane" illustrator, Keith Ward, and at the Otis/Parsons School of Design in Los Angeles, California.

In 1985, Rod Cameron founded East/West Arts, Inc., a design and art studio in Ventura, California. His work has been shown on major network television and has received 17 awards for illustrative excellence.